A Guide for Creating and Enjoying Inspi[ring]
Experiences by Terry Stevens with A[...]

The Spark
and a Sense of
Wonder

For the curious, the wanderers and the storytellers.

GRAFFEG

ACKNOWLEDGEMENTS

We have authored this book for everyone, but especially for YOU. Thank you for taking time to read this book. We encourage you to think carefully about the future of our communities and the way they interact with tourists and visitors.

We have been inspired by those who are referenced in these pages. We are indebted to our sponsors and supporters. We acknowledge the skills of the design team at Graffeg.

Sculpture *Haizearen Orrazia/Peine del Viento* by Eduardo Chillida, San Sebastian, Spain. Photo: Shutterstock.

The Institute of Re-imagined Places & Experiences

SUPPORTERS

CONTENTS

Preface by the Curators   6

1. **Welcome** from our Supporters   8
2. **The Trendsetters and Thought Leaders** as Our Guest Contributors   16
   - Nancy Davies, Chief Creative Director Global Wellness Summit (USA)   16
   - Tim Rusby, FRSA. Founder, The Visitor Attraction Company (England)   17
   - Sara Mair Belshaw, Founder, Slow Adventure (Scotland)   18
   - Christina Pastor, Co-founder, NJOY Catalonia (Catalonia)   19
   - Claus Sendlinger, Founder, SLOWNESS (Portugal)   21
   - Mary McKeon, Tourism Officer, Mid-Ulster Council (N. Ireland)   22
   - Claus Rex, Tourism Chief, Visit Odsherred, (Denmark)   23
   - Tim O'Donoghue, Founder, Riverwind Foundation (USA)   24
   - Harry John, Founder, Pure Solutions, (Switzerland)   25
3. **The Why?** An Introduction by Terry Stevens and Alan Sandry   26
4. **The Essence of Psychogeography, Tourism and Sense of Place** An essay by Alan Sandry   30
5. **The Anatomy of a Great Experience** by Terry Stevens   32
6. **Food for Thought From Our Experts**   34
7. **Be Inspired by These Words**   45
8. **The Curated Collection of Great Experiences**   46
9. **The Institute of Re-imagined Places & Experiences* Inaugural Hall Of Fame 2025**   78
10. **My Back Pages** – Some Final Thoughts by Terry Stevens   89
11. **The Resources** (a great listen and a good read)   91

*A fictional think-tank encouraging innovation in creating a new generation of unique locally-based tourist experiences to counter the AI and VR epidemics that are eroding our ability to connect with real people in real places through deep interaction stirring real emotions.

WELCOME TO
The Imaginarium

Swimming in the Rhine, Rheinschwimmen, Basel. Photo: Basel Turismus.

Kites on Rindby Strand, Fanø Island, Denmark.
Photo: Visit Fanø.

PREFACE BY THE CURATORS

'Put there just a spark: ignite curiosity.'
Freeman Tilden, *Interpreting Our Heritage*, 1957.

'Didn't I come to bring you a sense of wonder'
Van Morrison, *Sense of Wonder*, 1985.

This book is an evocation and celebration of tourist experiences that delight and capture the imagination of those involved – both the guest and the host. These experiences talk to the whole person (the mind, body and the soul). They ignite a spark of curiosity and create a sense of wonder. They are rooted in the principles of psychogeography; they embrace a sense of place and are delivered with a human touch.

They are the antidote to technology-based digital experiences.

In these pages, we explore the concept of psychogeography and have invited experts to give their insights into experience development. We examine the anatomy and make-up of a great experience and explore examples of best practice from around the world.

We give you the tools and rules for playing this new game. We suggest a musical playlist and some pertinent quotes to whet your creative instincts. We suggest a reading list to further your understanding of how it's done. Finally, we have created the inaugural Institute of Re-imagined Places & Experiences 'Hall of Fame', with 18 original thinkers and influencers.

In a global tourism industry increasingly characterised by sameness, this book has been inspired by those people in the 'Hall of Fame', as well as organisations and destinations that choose to walk another path, for example:

- The Institute for Psychogeographic Adventure (www.ipaexperiments.com)

- LATOUREX. LAboratoire de TOURisme EXpérimental · LABoratory of EXperimental TOURism · LAboratorio di TUrismo SPERimentale. (www.latourex.org)

- Le projet des Machines de l'île est à la croisée des « mondes inventés » de Jules Verne, de l'univers de Léonard de Vinci et du passé industriel de Nantes (www.lesmachines-nantes.fr)

- The Slovenian Tourist Board's SUE (Slovenian Unique Experiences) (www.slovenia.info)

- Examples of wonderful experiences encountered in many destinations around the world with special mention to what is happening in Istria (Croatia), Austria, Denmark, Italy, Canada and Norway

- Destination Canada (2024) *Tourism's Wealth & Well-being Index: a new way to measure tourism's impact in Canadian communities.* (www.tourismdatacollective.ca)

- World Experience Organisation's *Remarkable 2025: The Shape of Experiential Art & Entertainment* by Laura Hess of Reuleaux (www.worldxo.org)

- The work of hybrid thinkers such as Something & Son (www.somethingandson.com), Gordon Young – especially the Comedy Carpet in Blackpool, England (www.gordonyoung.info) with Andy Altman of Why Not Associates (www.whynotassociates.com)

- The Institute of Imagination (www.ioi.london)

- Freeman Tilden's pioneering book *Interpreting Our Heritage* (1957).

- The Creative Environment for Creative Leadership programmes at IEDC Bled Centre of Management, Bled (www.iedc.si)

One of the originals who recognised the fundamental impact of the shift to experiences and the unique celebration of sense of place in the hospitality sector was the effervescent founder and former CEO of Design Hotels, Claus Sendlinger. However, Sendlinger was clear that the tourism industry needs innovative and creative ideas to survive but the industry is not sufficiently innovative or creative to deliver the experiences needed – 'We need hybrid thinkers to deliver hybrid solutions.' He urges us to engage with different disciplines and to be bold and creative. His new project, SLOWNESS (www.slowness.com), is striving to deliver bold, creative experiences with a sense of purpose.

This sentiment is echoed in the words of another one of our 'Hall of Famers', Manfred Grubauer, who fears that the tourism industry has lost the creative engine that was fuelled by personalities. He says, 'At this time tourism needs personalities that our successors can look to for inspiration and bravery. Too many in the tourism industry are unsettled and turn away from the wonderful genre of tourism to sink into the anonymity of administration. May the personalities that created the experiences that are celebrated in this book be role models for future tourism professionals.'

Personalities are important. We must avoid anonymity. Every destination needs a personality and a face behind every tourism plan, and especially the curation of visitor experiences.

1. WELCOME FROM OUR SUPPORTERS

Fáilte Feirste Thiar. Photo: Visit West Belfast.

FÁILTE FEIRSTE THIAR/VISIT WEST BELFAST
by Harry Connolly, Executive Director, Fáilte Feirste Thiar/ Visit West Belfast (www.visitwestbelfast.com)

Fáilte Feirste Thiar (Welcome to West Belfast) took the opportunity arising from peace to develop the West Belfast tourism product, develop the tourism infrastructure, support tourism-related businesses and social enterprises, train local people as tour guides and promote local social and economic regeneration via small business development and job creation.

We market the uniqueness of West Belfast as a tourist attraction, rebranding the area as a place to visit which provides quality tourism experiences and customer satisfaction.

West Belfast has embraced a unique approach to community tourism by focusing on its rich history, culture and activism. Through guided tours, local storytelling and heritage sites, it offers an authentic experience that highlights the area's resilience and identity, fostering both education and economic growth within the community. Fáilte Feirste Thiar acts as a role model, a leader and living example in what can be achieved when local communities work collaboratively and in partnership with Government departments, tourism promoters and other stakeholders to create employment and opportunities and contribute to the portrayal of an image of a community – confident, welcoming and vibrant.

SLOVENIAN TOURIST BOARD by MSc. Maja Pak Olaj, Director (www.slovenia.info)

Slovenia is more than a destination – it's a feeling. Through Slovenia Unique Experiences, we invite guests to step off the beaten path and discover boutique adventures that awaken the senses, create meaningful connections and leave lasting impressions. Rooted in sustainability and authenticity, these carefully curated experiences enrich both visitors and local communities. This is the heart of the 'I feel Slovenia' brand – an invitation to not just explore but to truly feel our nature, culture and hospitality. I feel Slovenia.

I feel LOVE.
May this manual inspire you to craft experiences that resonate long after they end.

Goriska Brda, Slovenia.
Photo: Slovenian Tourist Board.

CATALAN TOURIST BOARD by Patrick Torrent Quell, Executive Director, Catalan Tourist Board (www.act.gencat.cat)

When Catalonia founded the Network of European Regions for Competitive and Sustainable Tourism (NECSTouR) in 2007, together with Tuscany and Provence-Alpes-Côte d'Azur, it set itself the goal of ensuring that the voices of European destinations committed to a responsible tourism model would be heard within the European institutions.

After all these years, the content of this book confirms that the seed of commitment to the region and local communities has germinated in many diverse destinations.

The challenge today has evolved. Catalonia is addressing the climate emergency by responding to the commitment it made when it signed the 2024 Glasgow Declaration through its *Climate Action Plan for Tourism*.

At the same time, it is developing a new marketing strategy aimed at transforming the visitor economy into a factor in the regeneration of communities' productive models. Thus, the social sustainability of tourism becomes a priority and requires the involvement of residents in their triple role: as recipients, planners and producers. We aspire to welcome conscious visitors who value our uniqueness as a community and truly become temporary residents, with rights but also obligations. Similarly, we hope that residents can enjoy the enormous diversity of attractions that Catalonia offers year-round, making our destination a better place to live, because only then can it aspire to become a better place to visit.

Above: Hikers taking a route through the Long Lake within the Aigüestortes and Sant Maurici National Park. Photo: Gonzalo Azumendi. © Agència Catalana de Turisme.

REPUCON by Mark O'Connell, Founder and CEO (www.repucon.ie)

In many respects, when Maya Angelou said, 'I've learned that people will forget what you said, people will forget what you did, but people will never forget how you made them feel', she was really looking into the future of tourism experiences. Every level of analysis, from visitor motivations to global tourism trends, repeatedly highlights the insatiable appetite for authentic and immersive experiences with the local person telling the local story. Our research repeatedly highlights the direct links between the level of visitor interaction in experience delivery and the corresponding satisfaction ratings. We refer to it as the Tourism Experience Pulse™ (TEP – devised by Repucon Consulting and Stevens & Associates).

The TEP charts the correlation between the level of human interaction in experience delivery, experience quality, visitor satisfaction and revenue generation. It goes beyond functional attention to customer service and reinforces how we must consider our approach to experience development. It's a simple lesson for businesses and destinations. By stimulating the senses and the pulse of the visitor through the excitement of the personal interaction, the corresponding economic and satisfaction value increases. The willingness to engage with the visitor and place them at the centre of the experience respects the time-old traditions of hospitality and local storytelling. This book and its core message act as a timely reminder that tourism can never lose sight of this. Never forget how you make them feel!

Below: The Barrack Street Mural, Ennis by Eva Mena, Bilbao. Photo: Terry Stevens.

The Adriatic Hotel, Rovinj.
Photo: Maistra Hospitality Group.

MAISTRA HOTELS GROUP by Tomislav Popović, President of the Maistra Management Board (www.maistra.com)

The Maistra Hospitality Group (part of the Adris Group and one of the leading Croatian tourism companies), is known for its high-quality hotels, resorts and camps in the most attractive Croatian destinations – Dubrovnik, Rovinj, Vrsar, Zagreb and (soon) Split. The Group is dedicated to setting new standards in delivering unique guest experiences. This philosophy permeates all aspects of the company's interface with their guests – exquisite design at every touchpoint, carefully selected artworks adorning public spaces, the impeccable use of local produce and the highly sought-after collection of 15 Maistra Unique Experiences. These include a private dinner surrounded by the magnificent Roman amphitheatre in Pula, a discovery tour of Istria's award-winning olive oil and personal time with a truffle hunter. The Hotel Adriatic, located in the historic centre of Rovinj, exemplifies the Maistra approach – a rare hotel in which the artwork was created exclusively for it, creating a compelling collection of over 100 unique works of art. Istrian gastronomy experiences abound, especially with Grand Park's Agli Amici Rovinj earning its second Michelin star and three Maistra Collection restaurants receiving Michelin recommendations, Cap Aureo, Tekka by Lone and Wine Vault – Levante Edition. This dedication to local, seasonal and high-quality ingredients is also captured in *Flavours of Istria*, a special monograph featuring 15 recipes from Cap Aureo and chef Jeffrey Vella, reflecting the four seasons and the peninsula's four types of soil. The book is available in Cap Aureo, the signature restaurant of the Grand Park, and Park Concept Store on Lungomare Plaza.

VISIT BELFAST by Rachael McGuickin, Deputy CEO and Director of Business Development, Sustainability and Transformation, Visit Belfast (www.visitbelfast.com)

Belfast is a city that confounds expectations and rewards curiosity. As the happiest city in the UK, our hearts are big, our character stout, our humour dark and our craic mighty. For visitors there's the unforgettable experience of being in a city in transition – an edgy city that's on the move. Colourful, complicated, messy... and magnificent. Because Belfast is a city that's rich in so many ways. Richly storied: an early coastal settlement named Béal Feirste, famous for *Titanic*, enfolded by hills, rivers and loughs, this is a place with a long and complex history, a tapestry of narratives, and now a new story in the making. Belfast has long been home to creators who dare to dream – industrial designers and innovators, technicians and craftspeople, as well as artists, writers, musicians and filmmakers. Our city is brimming with passionate tourism and hospitality entrepreneurs who dared to believe that if you build it, they will come – and they do, in their droves!

Tourism is genuinely loved here. It is such an important part of our story, and as a result there's a generosity and kindness to strangers that can take the visitor by surprise, and that's part of the city's charm.

At Visit Belfast, we are delighted to support this book. Its main author, Terry Stevens, has always challenged us to create, innovate, be brave, be bold and be different. This book is a celebration of just that, and you cannot help but be inspired by it.

Top: Rachael McGuickin. Photo: Rachael McGuickin.

Belfast pottery plaque, Cathedral Quarter, Belfast. Photo: Terry Stevens.

KITZBÜHEL TOURISMUS by Dr. Viktoria Veider-Walser, CEO of Kitzbühel Tourismus (www.kitzbuehel.com)

Wandering in Kitzbühel. Photo: Kitzbühel Tourismus.

Tradition is not a constraint, but a foundation for innovation.

A great experience in Kitzbühel comes from a special mix of tradition, quality and forward thinking. While it's famous for winter sports, Kitzbühel is much more than that – it's a place people love to visit all year round. In fact, almost half of the guests come in summer, drawn by the town's charm and the variety of experiences on offer.

The philosophy is clear: experiences must be meaningful, timeless and adaptable – not defined by demographics like age, but by shared values and expectations. Kitzbühel does not merely adapt to trends; it integrates them in a way that honours its legacy, from its 750-year-old old town to its pioneering infrastructure and cultural landmarks.

The town's unique identity lies in its seamless juxtaposition of contrasts – prestige and authenticity, grandeur and tranquility, natural escape and urban flair. Whether through large-scale sporting events or serene moments at sacred places like the Klosterkirche chapel, every guest can find their personal highlight.

Ultimately, what makes Kitzbühel exceptional is its ability to offer genuine, deeply rooted experiences that are both reflective and progressive – an Alpine destination where time-honoured charm meets contemporary lifestyle.

Become a shepherd for a day in the Basque Region.
Photo: Tourism Euskadi.

Traditional festival in Bregenzerwald.
Photo: Andreas Haller.

2. THE TRENDSETTERS AND THOUGHT LEADERS AS OUR GUEST CONTRIBUTORS

Nancy Davies, Chief Creative Officer and Executive Director, Global Wellness Summit. Founder and President of the Global Wellness Institute (www.globalwellnesssummit.com; www.globalwellnessinstitute.org)

Photo: Nancy Davies.

I wear a watch that needs winding. I write with a fountain pen. I still love the texture and depth of tone of images captured on a film camera. I collect antique manual typewriters and dial telephones. There is something about the tactile sensation, the clicking sounds and the satisfaction of engaging with buttons and dials and metal surfaces that I find reassuring. That unmistakable scratch of a needle on a record album, spinning on a turntable. The romanticism of these objects are a part of my everyday life.

So where might someone like me go to experience wellness in a way that resonates? I go to Central Park in New York City. In Central Park I marvel at, and photograph, the flowering trees lining various paths. I sit in the Shakespeare Garden and read poetry. I play on the swings with my grandchildren at any number of embedded playgrounds, or perhaps a few spins on the carousel. I paddle a boat across a pond, admiring the fathers and sons who are launching tiny, carefully hand-crafted boats into the water. I buy an ice-cream cone from a street-cart vendor who has been part of the park for decades. I see the imposing skyline, ringing the park from almost every angle, but the tall, stern stone and glass buildings are reduced to a shadowy rim, pushed into the background. The full force of nature is the central point of my wellbeing, the central place for thinking and walking. The Central Park.

Central Park was designed by Frederick Law Olmsted and Calvery Vaux and built with the human experience at its core. It was meant to be a place to escape, for a little while, the harsh realities of a bustling, noisy city. It was conceived in the 1850s, but its purpose is as relevant today, and it is a prime example of a place designed for the wellbeing of those who enter.

Tim Rusby FRSA, Founder and CEO, The Visitor Attraction Company (www.thevisitorattractioncompany.com)

Photo: Tim Rusby.

Whenever I catch myself flipping through visitor attraction industry trade journals, dazzled by the latest tech-laden 'immersive experiences', a small voice in my head always chimes in: 'Think more Keith.' Keith 'Sparky' Sparks was a creative powerhouse and one of the UK's original visitor attraction imagineers. His infectious philosophy was simple yet profound: 'A good story, well told. Keep it simple, for the child in all of us. Be the purveyors of memories, not stuff, and hold a mirror to the place.'

These were the guiding principles, forming the foundation of unforgettable, engaging and joyful experiences, and although he was no luddite, he looked on technology as a tool to be used with caution – an occasional means, never an end.

As a counterbalance to the surge of tech-heavy attractions, here are some of my favourite lower-tech projects, both old and new – the kind Sparky would wholeheartedly applaud.

1. Adventure Play at Windsor Great Park is one of the most enchanting play spaces ever created. This award-winning masterpiece was designed and built for the Crown Estate and combines artistry, engineering and a touch of magic, using natural hardwood sourced from the Windsor Estate. Beyond the impressive playscape, the meticulously designed amenities for parents show an extraordinary attention to detail. Seamlessly nestled within its surroundings, this place left me awestruck.

2. Dennis Severs' House, Spitalfields is part theatre, part historic home, part museum – and entirely free of technology. This immersive experience takes visitors through 10 rooms of a Georgian townhouse from London's East End once owned by Dennis Severs. Designed by Dennis as a 'historical imagination' of a Huguenot silk weaver family's life, each room feels alive with incidental moments. The combination of scenography, historic interiors, art and meticulous set dressing creates what Severs called a 'still life drama'. Walking through with an actor guide who never breaks character is utterly mesmerising. For an even more profound experience, try the silent or candlelit tours.

3. Villa Ventorum at The Newt in Somerset is an exquisite 'still life drama'. This recreation of a fourth-century Romano-British villa offers an astonishingly detailed glimpse into the past. Every element, both inside and out, is crafted to perfection. It feels as if the occupants have just stepped out, with 1,700 years dissolving in an instant. Remarkably, the entire space is technology-free – not even artificial lighting is used to highlight the ornate interiors. It is more than just a set; it is an extraordinary immersive journey through time.

In a world increasingly enamoured with high-tech attractions, these projects stand as a testament to the power of simplicity, storytelling and human connection.

Sara Mair Belshaw, Founder of Slow Adventure (www.slow-adventure.com)

Photo: Sara Mair Belshaw.

The benefits of nature-based activities are well documented in terms of health, and the slow pace of human-powered travel lends itself beautifully to being able to enjoy your surroundings, observe wildlife and engage with the local community.

Carefully crafted adventures are authentic, regenerative holidays that give the guests the opportunity to really become part of the place that they are travelling through. When customers book a trip on our online platform, they also choose an impact project local to their holiday. A donation of 5% goes directly to projects that care for the local areas that are home to our adventures. With the impact fund, we support, restore and regenerate beautiful wild places so that we can create a better balance between people and nature and visitors and locals.

Local communities are the backbone of Slow Adventure because they create and deliver the adventures and suggest the local impact projects. We stand alongside business owners who share the slow adventure ethos to reduce our impact, those who create the warmest of welcomes and embody a connection with their community that can be shared with slow adventurers.

Travel and tourism can be a force for good, but there needs to be a fundamental shift in the way in which this extractive industry is developed and managed. Slow Adventure chose to create a system where customers donate each time they book because we fundamentally believe in paying to support the main attraction – nature and culture! This is about system change and a collective responsibility – not just our customers, but every customer, business and government that benefits from the main attraction.

Our customers say that the reason they choose to adventure with us is because they can support a project that is local and relevant to where they adventure, and because they know where their donation goes. The fundamental part of their willingness to pay is transparency. It's time for the entire tourism sector to join the movement to opt in so that generations to come can continue to enjoy these extraordinary wild places.

Cristina Pastor, Co-founder with Claire Aubertel of NJOY CATALONIA (www.njoycatalonia.com)

NJOY CATALONIA works on creating unique experiences based on three fundamental pillars: authenticity, originality and sustainability.

Its philosophy focuses on connecting people with the most genuine essence of Catalonia, offering experiences that combine tradition, innovation and respect for the environment. Authenticity is at the heart of every experience. We seek to highlight the cultural, historical and natural richness of the region, allowing visitors to immerse themselves in the true Catalan identity. From exploring unique landscapes to participating in local activities, every detail reflects the passion for preserving the roots and essence of this territory.

Originality is manifested in the creation of personalised and surprising proposals, designed to make a difference. We are committed to unconventional experiences capable of awakening emotions, curiosity and wonder. Each activity is carefully designed to offer unforgettable and exceptional moments.

Finally, sustainability is at the core of all its actions. Our philosophy promotes responsible tourism that respects and protects the environment while promoting the development of local communities. From choosing local suppliers to integrating eco-friendly practices, its commitment to sustainability ensures that experiences have a positive impact on both nature and people. We combine these three essential values to create experiences that not only enrich those who enjoy them but also contribute to the well-being of the environment and the community. Each experience is an invitation to discover Catalonia in a profound, respectful and unique way.

Photo: Cristina Pastor and Claire Aubertel.

Slowness was born out of an intention, a wish, a recourse – the need to reframe the way we live and interact.

Photo: Clemens Poloczek.

Claus Sendlinger, formerly founder and CEO of Design Hotels and now founder of SLOWNESS (www.slowness.com)

Born out of Intention

Slowness was born out of an intention, a wish, a recourse – the need to reframe the way we live and interact. Today we are opening the doors of our first fully fledged Slowness habitat, our Flussbad campus in Berlin, where we are materialising everything we have learned from a decade of tracking the artists, travelers and navigators of cultural undercurrents that best describe a new and more satisfying way of living. The question is: what kind of life becomes possible when we explore other registers of pace?

To be slow is not just about decreasing the speed of life. It's about taking the time to reconsider our actions and think more deeply and responsibly about how we live. We want to nourish ourselves on what Thoreau called 'the tonic of wildness' and live more often in the moment, opening it up to something 'more elastic, more starry, more immortal'. In other words, we are talking about perception.

At Slowness, we are carefully re-examining the ordinary elements of hospitality in order to invite this state of wonder. For us, narrative is driven by curation. At the heart of our Berlin campus, we set out to build a contemporary temple for sonic arts and ended up with an architectural marvel that we called Reethaus. Our programme there is developed in tandem with Soundwalk Collective and MONOM, two of the outfits most responsible today for pushing the envelope of what music can be. At Reethaus, we are experiencing music as healing, with a calendar of spatial sound and drone music installations deliberately calibrated for their medicinal effects. We are positing architecture as a frame for life-centered exchange, and we are developing new modern rituals as a way to restore our sense of time and bring about community. The story of Flussbad spins out from there.

I believe that in the future values will become more important than brands as such. Every industry will have to realign to offer the world what it is deeply longing for – wonder, a pace adequate to the human animal, and the deep meaning we all desire and that a century of materialism has proven is irreplaceable.

Building Flussbad was a radical decision to lend brick-and-mortar weight to this philosophy. We gave ourselves the freedom to let *slowness* – the concept, aesthetic and ethic – express itself at every scale. Teams of architects and sound designers, material scientists and scent artists have come together to advance the art and science of distilling presence at our new campus on the Spree.

From this carefully considered space, we are preparing to launch an annual conference and a school at Flussbad, an open-source programme of inspiration and innovation that will serve to connect our peers to each other and to this emerging paradigm. Slowness, more than a company, is a movement, and every movement needs a school.

Flussbad is an ambitious project that combines world-leading design with a keen sense of the needs and potentials of the contemporary human. In many regards we may be ahead of our time – but at the same time we know the world can't wait. We can no longer wait for slow.

Mary McKeown, Tourism Officer, Mid-Ulster Council, Northern Ireland (www.omdarksky.com)

Beaghmore Star Trail, the Sperrin Mountains.

'Reconnect with the stars above' evokes a beautiful sense of wonder and reflection.

It always suggested to me to take a moment to pause, look up at the night sky and reflect on the vastness of the universe. As a child I always spent my summers in the foothills of the Sperrins, meandering through the fields and stumbling upon Beaghmore Stone Circles, a Neolithic site dating back more than 5000 years.

I would stand in awe and wonder why our ancestors placed them as they did. My personal opinion was that they were mimicking what was happening in the sky above, because as the night fell, the site and the sky came alive with the Milky Way, stars and planets appearing in front of my naked eye. That was when I knew this place was special and I needed to tell the world about it. I needed to tell them about OM Dark Sky Park and Observatory and leave a legacy for our next generation to enjoy this special place, which is now filled with giants, telescopes and solar walks.

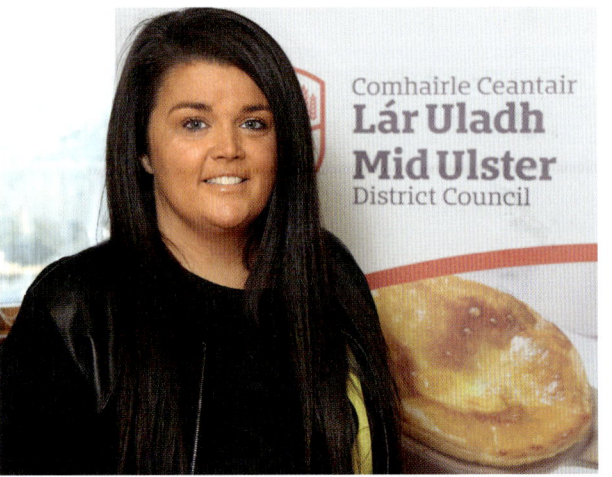

Photos Mid-Ulster Council.

Claus Rex, Tourist Chief, Visit Odsherred, Denmark (www.visitodsherred.com)

Let's be completely personal here… how do we provide the best visitor experience? A complex question, not least because there is often a gap between how we design experiences and what actually works. I will give you two examples of special experiences that moved me while they were happening which I still remember, and which I found to be genuine, human and in alignment with the place where they occurred.

The 10 tastings of Skopje, North Macedonia is a tour that goes behind the façade of a city that often has the character of being a backdrop. The tour takes the visitor to a local guide's favourite spots, ensures they taste all local specialties and at the same time creates a contrasting narrative about a city that otherwise delivers a constructed story – and thus serves as a mirror.

Sunset song at the Vippefyr (fire beacon), Skagen, Denmark is organised by a local opera singer as a recurring concert and communal singing event throughout the summer. The bright nights of Scandinavia are celebrated while guests sing along and the area's history, landscape, song heritage and melancholy are honoured.

Both experiences will probably be unknown to the reader, just as they will never make it to official lists of experiences – like many other similar products around the world. The reason I reference them are (i) they are tied to their place and history; (ii) they are supported by strong personalities with love for and understanding of their area; and (iii) they move people and are genuine.

Neither originate from experience design, nor are they scalable or overly commercial. Despite this, their inherent power lies in creating memories and the feeling of belonging – even if just for a day.

Destinations in the future will compete to be the ones that create the strongest bonds with their guests and develop the strongest, most unique and most place-based memories. The cursed duty of the destination developer becomes ensuring that there is a portfolio of emotionally charged experiences, while the commercial aspect of the experience increasingly turns into infrastructure and is not what carries the important part of the stay. Dare we move down this path and go to the core of the human experience? I hope so.

Photo: Claus Rex.

Tim O'Donoghue, sustainable and regenerative tourism specialist, Founder of Riverwind Foundation, Global Manager of The Long Run

Photo: Tim O'Donoghue.

The core of great visitor experiences is connection. Connection is with locals, local communities and cultures, fellow travellers and nature. These connections are powerful when they are genuine, immersive and meaningful. The power of such experiences is often amplified by their novelty and spontaneity.

The Human Connection: a highlight for many visitors is meeting, listening to and learning from locals. They may be park rangers, guides, community members and other educators and storytellers. Such connections are facilitated when the circumstances of the travel experience provide opportunities for interaction with locals. While travel agencies, tour operators and destination marketing companies can offer an array of experiences, the traveller must discern what's truly genuine and not commercialised, staged, or culturally appropriated. There is something deeply affirming when we experience a mind- and soul-satisfying connection with another person across cultures, languages and nationalities. Perhaps we are reminded of our common humanity and to appreciate the diversity of expression within our commonality. As one indigenous person shared with me, if we want world peace, we must come to know and respect one another. Travel is a path to world peace.

The Nature Connection: the primary reason visitors come to my neck of the woods is the abundant wildlife, pristineness of the environment and stunning scenery. The multigenerational work of conservationists has been critical in sustaining and restoring the integrity of nature. Whether it is a walk in the frontcountry or hike into the backcountry of Jackson Hole or Yellowstone, the visitor can leave behind the complexities and distractions in life and enter into a sensory experience of place. Nature breathes calm into our nervous system, slows down our mind and invites wonder to be part of our experience. Nature is a tuning fork that reconnects us with our authentic self.

My Happy Place

The popularity of long walks or pilgrimages is increasing. More nations and regions of the world are creating these cultural, physical and spiritual adventures, whether they are weeks or months long. I've had climactic experiences by walking the Camino de Santiago in Spain (Way of St. James), Via di Francesco in Italy (Way of St. Francis), Via Podiensis in France (French Way of St. James) and Dingle Way in Ireland. Walking reduces the barriers to connect with locals and nature and creates paths to life-enhancing and even life-changing experiences. Rather than travelling by car or coach and staying in hotels, Janet and I realised how much easier it is for locals and us to connect when we move more slowly through communities and landscapes, stay in hostels and B&Bs and share communal meals.

The novelty and spontaneity of daily experiences holds us in the moment and slows down time.

Harry John, Head of Pure Solutions and Head of Markets, St Elmo's Tourism (www.saint-elmos.travel)

Photo: Harry John.

This is why tourism and hospitality are so precious: human contact based on mutual respect in combination with touching emotions.

Hospitality. Made with heart. The world is complicated enough. Tourism and hospitality should be simple and authentic. It can also be a contribution to international understanding, as well as peace-making. The more the world is getting globalised, the more people like to feel the simple things of life. A warm welcome with a smile, a nice surprise, enjoying the moment, sharing emotions with family and friends. Of course, the culinary delights are a delicious way to discover a country.

When writing these words, my first steps in hospitality and tourism come into my mind. It started with summer jobs serving food and drinks whilst talking to guests and all kinds of services, then education in tourism management and over the years working in DMOs, such as Lausanne, Montreux Riviera and the canton of Berne. It all made me enjoy the human touch of hospitality even more.

I'm the third generation of our family to work in tourism. My grandfather would tell me his experiences as a gardener in five-star hotels, and what a personal and happy moment it always was! Many of the guests would come from the UK and spend the summer enjoying the hotel, flowers and gardens.

This is why tourism and hospitality are so precious: human contact based on mutual respect in combination with touching emotions. It's an inspiration and satisfaction to make new experiences and friends. Simple and made with heart. That's what hospitality is all about! Last but not least, and most importantly: travelling and exploring can definitely make us humble again.

Carreg Samson, North Pembrokeshire, Wales. Photo: The Retreats Group.

3. THE WHY? AN INTRODUCTION BY TERRY STEVENS AND ALAN SANDRY

In the highly competitive global marketplace, tourism destinations are continually searching for innovative ideas that deliver unique, value-added, experiences that have strong appeal for their guests, involve tourism businesses and engage positively with the host community.

Increasingly, destinations are being seduced by new technologies delivering augmented and virtual realities to achieve these goals. The QR, AI, CR and AR code and robots are rapidly replacing the 'human touch'. Far from enriching the tourist experience, these technologies are diluting any emotional connection between the place, the people and the culture of a destination.

Tourists are increasingly seeking the authentic (whatever that means), the real, the tangible, and the human interaction that comes from unique ways that a community can share its story. These types of experiences are not overly structured or organised. They tend to be much more organic, full of soul, and ooze a sense of place. They allow the guest to explore, to wander and to wonder.

This book celebrates carefully selected examples of these types of experiences – the antidote to technology-based and overly planned experiences – and the wonderful personalities that curate them. Our hope is to inspire others to explore the rich opportunities that exist to create wonderfully emotional and profound experiences by harnessing different ways to connect the guest to the host community.

We look to psychogeography as our building block. Merlin (also the name of the mythical magician in the legends of King Arthur – so good name for this topic) Coverley tells us that psychogeography is 'strangely familiar but no one seems quite to pin down exactly what it means or where it comes from.' The term can be traced back to the 1950s when, under Guy Debord, it became a tool for attempting to transform urban life. Debord defined it as 'the study of the specific effects of the geographical environment, consciously organised or not, on the emotional behaviour of individuals.'

It is a concept that is a means of exploring behavioural impacts of a place and is therefore relevant to both the citizen and the tourist/visitor – who is in reality merely a temporary resident.

Psychogeography is the point where psychology and geography intersect. In many ways the literary traditions of a society are the precursors to psychogeography. We can all reference a writer or a poet from our neck of the woods whose words capture the essence of the place. For me it would be the Dorset (England) poet and novelist Thomas Hardy, and for Alan it would be the Welsh poet from Swansea, Dylan Thomas.

Thomas' description of his 'ugly, lovely town' in *Reminiscenses of Childhood* is non-linear in style and its presentation full of local history, fact, fiction and personal detail: 'as a crawling, sprawling, slummed, unplanned, jerry-villa'd, and smug suburbed, by the side of a long and splendid curving shore, where truant boys and Sandfield boys and old anonymous men, in the tatters and hangovers of a hundred charity suits, beachcombed, idled and paddled'. Simply brilliantly evocative, and you can all imagine the place.

Thomas De Quincey (1785–1859) escaped Manchester for Wales but is best known for his drug-fuelled ramblings through London, which afforded him new

The Oyster King, Fanø Island. Photo: Robert Attermann.

ways of experiencing the familiar and the unfamiliar. These otherworldly insights are captured in his 1821 book *Confessions of an English Opium-Eater* (opium was at the time a legal substance). We are not advocating that you encourage your visitors to adopt such practices, however, it is interesting to note the rise of cannabis and CBD tours around the world – perhaps Thomas De Quincy was onto something 200 years ago?

It was another Welsh writer who, in the 1930s, recognised the power of slowing down to get to know a place. Wandering was Arthur Machen's preferred mode. He was significantly influenced by the 'enchanted landscape of Wales' and the fact that the curious with 'a trained eye can reveal the eternal behind the common place.' For Iain Sinclair (1997), walking through a place reveals that it is a helpful process for planning tourist experiences.

Walking, or preferably wandering or sauntering, implies the idea of the *flâneur*, whose aimless walking is elevated to an art form. Indeed, as the erstwhile county planning officer Graham King (a self-professed *flâneur*) wrote in a personal communication, 'from the urban or the rural wanderer to the armchair traveller, from the derive (an unplanned walk with constant reflection) to the detournement (the hijacking of a visitor to do something different to that planned), psychogeography provides us with new ways of apprehending our surroundings transforming the familiar of our everyday experiences into something new and unexpected.' He goes on to highlight the importance of diversity – 'it is the order of the day' – and the celebration of variety rather than binary connections that all too often define a visitor experience. Diverging scenes will, according to King, allow the mind to produce different thoughts and conclusions. The approach is always poetic and refreshing for the mind, the body, the spirit and the soul.

We return to Coverley to summarise the relevance of psychogeography to contemporary tourism. For Merlin, 'psychogeography speaks to the soul. It provides a template for fresh thinking about how we engage with our communities (and our guests).'

Robert MacFarlane, writing in the *Times Literary Supplement* (October 2005), gave us a glimpse of how to use psychogeography to create a unique visitor experience when he exhorted us to 'Unfold a street map. Place on it a glass, rim side down, anywhere on this map, and draw around the edge. Pick up the map, go out into the city (town or village) and walk the circle. Record the experience in whatever medium you favour.' It works. Try it!

Below: Swansea Botanic Gardens, Singleton Park.
Photo: Terry Stevens.

OUR MANIFESTO FOR THE FUTURE OF GREAT VISITOR EXPERIENCES IS SIMPLE:

We know digital drives awareness, knowledge and information. We know that the youthful markets dwell in a digital mind set. However, we wish to celebrate the enduring, powerful and meaningful experiences that do not rely upon digital enhancements.

- Great tourist experiences are often the antithesis of the digital.
- There is a need to get back to basics.
- Spontaneity and serendipity are vital ingredients of these experiences.
- Freedom to explore, to wander, to become inquisitive is vital.
- Happiness and pleasure are vital outcomes.
- Inspiration and joy come from local interactions.
- Accept that it is often a struggle to define the authentic.
- Many experiences are reassuringly hard to find.
- Nurture those tourists who care about the places they visit.
- Welcome the fact that tourist behaviour is shifting from 'nobody cares' to 'everybody cares'.
- Destinations have a pulse and tourists need to feel that heartbeat.
- Encourage visitors to walk and talk (with strangers).

Our recent research into tourism trends (supply and demand) reveals the following paradigm shifts that will shape the way we think about future tourist experiences:

- Hybridity is witnessed everywhere with the emergence of novel, innovative, 'who'd have thought it' ideas by hybrid thinkers putting together combinations of ideas that collide to create something very different.
- Co-creation is vital and should involve all the senses and multiple layers of different components to give a composite experience addressing the mind, body and soul. Increasingly, the consumer should be involved in the co-creation process, ensuring a highly personalised customised experience.
- Co-creation demands a culture of co-dependency with different suppliers working together.
- The expectation of value is constantly being recalibrated. Value is no longer measured in monetary terms alone but with consideration of visitor's interests, motivations, time availability, need for self-development, willingness to pay and a desire to give back to the place they are visiting.

Experiences are really only about the story of the place, the culture and the people told in a compelling, original, engaging and authentic way.

Photo: Terry Stevens Collection.

4. THE ESSENCE OF PSYCHOGEOGRAPHY, TOURISM AND A SENSE OF PLACE
AN ESSAY BY ALAN SANDRY

'Psychogeography is definitely not killing people in random locations, however, if I was an English Literature teacher, I might go psycho trying to decide if it needs a hyphen in its name!'
Liam Lynch, Square Pit, February 2025

Every day, especially when on holiday or visiting somewhere new, we walk, we talk, we look. But do we? Do we listen, smell, taste or touch our surroundings? Really? Do we? We certainly use our legs to propel ourselves and our mouths, when not eating, to utter words, sometimes of wisdom, but often not. But do we honestly look?

We look at our phones with their X and Facebook apps downloaded. We spend countless hours watching people doing silly things on TikTok and YouTube. But, to paraphrase Dylan Thomas, do we 'look out' – with glasses or without them – because we 'want to see'? Looking is key – the key from the eye to the mind and the key that opens countless doors.

The history of psychogeography goes back to the emergence of humankind out from the age of the ape and into the natural world of the hunter gatherers. Before we invented houses, books, cars, televisions and the other gadgets we take for granted, we were forced to use our legs to get from A to B. Sometimes, our earliest ancestors went from A to B but then continued onward to C and D, not knowing what lay at points C and D. They were the original psychogeographers.

Psychogeography is the art of the imagination bumping into the reality of the physical. It can be, and indeed should be, both instantaneous and long lasting.
It can, and does, provide those memories which are truly memorable. From the 18th century, with Jean Jacques-Rousseau's *Les rêveries du promeneur solitaire* (The Reveries of the Solitary Walker) to the contemporary 'ramble, stop, observe' descriptions of Iain Sinclair, psychogeographers seek to engage with the world around us in its most holistic and enlightening sense. In a theme park, for example, this wouldn't be just a ride on a roller coaster, with screams and squeals galore, but also recognising the nuts and bolts of the machinery, the colour of the paint, the smell of the diesel. Detail is everything and we should attain sensory pleasure from all that can be observed, rather than the glossy, plastic simulacra experiences that many wish to point us toward.

The artist André Stitt describes his walks, and even his cycle trips, as 'performative drifts', so psychogeography can have many vehicles or portals for access. Think of the time that you have looked out of a plane window at 37,000 feet and imagined yourself floating across the clouds below you (always easier if you have some psychedelic rock channelling through your headphones). Yes, it is that type of experience we are after. Psychogeography is cathartic.

So, to label yourself a psychogeographer tourist, visit a place, embrace its experiences – one of those mentioned in this publication, hopefully, or one of your choice – and undertake three tasks: talk with at least five people in different settings (at the harbour, on a hillside, at a roadside café, etc.), write a poem, draw a picture, leave a message – easily visible or partly concealed – for the inhabitants and for future travellers. Ultimately, express your thoughts in whichever way suits you. Live in the moment and reflect upon it. By doing that, you will be a fully paid-up member of the Psychogeography and Tourism Ensemble.

The Hereford Mappa Mundi, about 1300, Hereford Cathedral, England.
Photo: Terry Stevens.

4. THE ESSENCE OF PSYCHOGEOGRAPHY, TOURISM AND A SENSE OF PLACE

5. THE ANATOMY OF A GREAT EXPERIENCE BY TERRY STEVENS

'What makes life worth living? Many people argue that it is fulfilling experiences – characterised by feelings of joy and pleasure, positive relationships, and a sense of engagement with people and place), meaning and achievement.' (Filip and Pearce, 2014)

All journeys begin somewhere. The route taken is influenced by individuals who shape our sense of engagement and sense of place to ensure we have great experiences: a teacher, a colleague, a writer, a poet, a musician, a friend or a stranger.

These are a few of my influencers: (i) the Teacher – **Hugh Prudden,** an inspiring, rebellious psychogeographer; (ii) the Colleague – **Dr J Geraint Jenkins**, a curator of the lives of ordinary people; (iii) the Writer – **Thomas Hardy**, whose novels take you to the soul of Wessex; (iv) the Poet – **T. S. Eliot**, whose definition of culture resonates with our manifesto; (v) the Musician – **Mutter Slater**, my friend from school, a 21st-century balladeer and minstrel with Stackridge and The Mutter Slater Band, whose songs carry a sense of belonging: 'The meadows hum below the morning sun, the church bells stir the breaking day. The dew has gone and so redemption comes, as people bow their heads to pray.' ('Keep Me From Fear', (2003); and (vi) the Doer – **Ross Aitken**, the champion of the Coker Rope and Sail initiative.

Left: Ross Aitken, Chair, Coker Rope & Sail Trust, West Coker.
Photo: Coker Rope & Sail Trust Archive.

Write Down Your Personal List of Influencers

I have long admired the work of those who are willing to try something different. In his 1957 book *Outrage*, Ian Nairn made us rethink post-war Britain; Clare Gunn's *Vacationscape* (1972) urged the reimagining of tourist destinations; Jane Jacobs, Dolly Pile and Graham King advocated the principles of psychogeography in planning places, whilst the creative writer Sonia Overall has publicly challenged heritage attraction operators to adopt the principles of psychogeography.

In 2017, Overall spoke out: 'Follow the arrows, stop here, and read this panel. Look at this. Does it have to be like this? Visitors are inherently intrigued by the past, the narrative, and the poetic possibilities of a place. We need to awaken curiosity. Fire up the imagination and foster enquiry. Encourage attentive walking all informed by Psychogeographic principles – switch on the senses, find the unexpected.'

Do I want the free audio tour? No, thanks. Do I really need the clutter of signage? Make the shift from passive to active engagement and to new ways of seeing both the urban and rural environments.

Follow the approach suggested by Wrights and Sites (www.mis-guide.com) in their 2006 treatise *A Mis-guide to Anywhere*, which enthused about following your own shadow. Go to a war memorial with a friend or a stranger and read out loud the silent words and names.

Head off to Reifensberg in Bregenzerwald, Austria (www.bregenzerwald.at) and walk wildflower meadows barefoot, smell the flowers or sit in a mountain stream – the antidote to the hotel spa complex. This is medicine for the soul and your entire physical body. If you want to blend barefoot walking

Llyn Gwynant, Gwynedd, Wales.
Photo: Visit Wales.

with old healing traditions, check out the Bizauer Obermoos for a stroll through millennia-old mossy moorland starting in the village centre of Bizau.

Psychogeography encompasses praxis, challenging the pre-programmed provision, inherited thinking and inherent limitations of the majority of the ways we deliver tourist experiences. We need to be more pirate. This is a time to rewrite the rules. Don't just question the status quo. It is time to make a difference for our guests and our communities.

In the words of Sam Conniff Allende (www.bemorepirate.com), 'Pirates faced up to a self-interested establishment, operating a broken system. They deployed innovative strategies to change the way things were done. They took happiness seriously.'

By following this path and rethinking the way we treat our guests, the outcomes will be more organic and spontaneous; though harder to manage, the impacts will be more meaningful and profound – you know when you feel it, when you share it.

'It is through our engagement with place (and people) that our own human being is made real, but it is also through our engagement that place takes on a sense or significance of its own.' (Malpas, 2018).

This powerful, highly personalised outcome, derived from a well-crafted experience, as defined by Jeff Malpas, is echoed in Van Morrison's 'Tore down a la Rimbaud' from his 1985 album *Sense of Wonder*.

It is repeated in Morrison's 2025 collection of songs *Remembering Now*, about which Andrew Male writes that he (Morrison) realises that the days of wonder are not in the past or lying in ruins, they are in the moment. They are now.

Immanuel Kant (the influential 18th-century German philosopher) rarely travelled, but he clearly understood the 'why' of experiences. He said encounters with new cultures, landscapes and ways of life are the catalysts for personal growth and the cultivation of curiosity and a sense of wonder.

6. FOOD FOR THOUGHT FROM OUR EXPERTS

AUTHENTICITY AS A PROMISE: THE CHALLENGE AND REWARD OF CREATING UNFORGETTABLE EXPERIENCES
by Misa Novak, Founder of ALOHAS and Chair of the Slovenian Unique Experiences (SUE)

Since 2018, I have been deeply committed to Slovenian Unique Experiences (SUE), shaping its vision and defining the criteria that separate a truly exceptional experience from just another tourist activity. Authenticity is our foundation, but uniqueness – being truly one of a kind – is the essential entrance criterion for SUE. In a world where destinations compete with increasingly similar offerings, we seek the rare, the unrepeatable – the kind of moments that exist only in Slovenia.

The 'My Way' communication platform, part of the 'I Feel Slovenia' brand, reflects this philosophy. We don't manufacture experiences; we uncover and refine what is already extraordinary. That's why SUE, a collection managed by the Slovenian Tourist Board, treasures those that are raw, deeply personal and inseparable from Slovenia's cultural and natural identity. Take the hike with sheep salting in Jezersko – nowhere else can visitors follow an alpinist from a legendary Slovene mountaineering family, guiding a flock of Indigenous Jezersko–Solčava sheep up to pristine pastures to be salted – a ritual as old as the mountains themselves. This is not staged; it is a living tradition, and guests are invited to become a part of it.

Authenticity demands simplicity and truth, but uniqueness demands irreplaceability. That's why cycling or kayaking through the flooded tunnels of the Mežica mine belongs in SUE – where else in the world can you paddle through a centuries-old underground labyrinth, illuminated only by your headlamp? Slovenia's allure isn't in grandiose displays but in these quiet, unforgettable moments of genuine connection.

We care deeply about SUE because it is more than a collection of experiences. It is a promise – to travellers, to local communities and to Slovenia itself – that the stories we share with the world will always be authentic, unrepeatable and truly unforgettable.

We uncover and refine what is already extraordinary.

Slovenia Unique Experiences. Photo: Slovenian Tourist Board.

Loch Ness. Photo: Jacobite.

IT'S ALL ABOUT THE STORY by Willie Cameron, Co-Founder of the Cobbs Group and Highland of Scotland Ambassador

A few years ago, I had the privilege of addressing the Wales National Cultural Tourism Conference. One of the other speakers was Professor Frans Schouten (formerly of NHTV Breda, Netherlands). He listed the points that a modern tourist was looking for in a destination: something interesting, something unique, something meaningful, good interpretation, imagination and, finally, a 'bloody good story'. I have been blessed, as far as these criteria are concerned, in such a way that I have both a strong sense of place and a bloody good story to tell.

The Highlands of Scotland – Caledonia, Alba – is a foreboding place on the periphery of western Europe. It is a land once inhabited by hunter gatherers, invaded by Vikings, settled by Celtic tribes and developed under the Clan system. What a foundation. What a backstory for the visitor seeking something deeper, for that immersion into a place, to identify with the local people and to embrace sustainability. All of this before they get to explore the Jacobite heritage, the poetry of Burns, the skirl of the bagpipes and the sweet sound of the Gaelic language, and before they meet that specific sense of place – my homeland, my square mile, Loch Ness in the Great Glen, home to Nessie, one of the greatest mysteries and legends in the world.

An ancient landscape, an extraordinary culture, now subject to rewilding, renewal and reimagining and the ability to deliver new types of tourism experiences. Dig deep, research and you too will find the fertile ground of your sense of place and your bloody good story.

In Guardia Parade, Valletta, Malta.
Photo: Visit Malta.

A HYPHEN OR NOT by Liam Lynch, Founder of Square Pit

Psychogeography spans disciplines. It explores relationships between individuals and the physical, social and emotional landscapes they inhabit.
It asks the question how these environments directly affect our emotions, behaviours and perceptions of a place. Vital ingredients for touristic experiences. Destinations need a psycho-geographical (note the hyphen) action plan to:

(i) identify how environments influence emotional well-being, productivity and identity then integrating digital immersion with analogue serenity to address the paradox of hyper-connectivity and the craving for grounded experiences;

(ii) create leisure environments that enhance wellbeing, self-discovery and community through sensory engagement and inclusive design;

(iii) bridge the gap between digital escapism and physical presence.

Our new measures of success should be emotional impact assessments with our guests, community engagement levels and cross-disciplinary collaborations.

A NEW GENERATION OF GUIDES by Professor Georg Steiner, long-time tourism director of Linz Tourismus (Linz/Upper Austria), now lead on transformation and sustainable habitat development, redesigning tourism at the Catholic University of Eichstätt-Ingolstadt, Germany

'The people are the city, not the houses' – Pericles, c. 500 BC. Tourist programs are too focused on history, sights and points of interest. Is this how experiences are created? Many guided tours are characterised by imparting knowledge. The buildings are backdrops and the city's biography. Guests don't know anything different when they book a tour. My theory is that meeting is the new sightseeing.

The guide becomes the moderator, they make the connections to good conversations, to interesting people, to an authentic destination in which you can immerse yourself. The future no longer belongs to the guides who are merely Wikipedia on two legs, but to the moderator, the host who presents their destination – not sterilely, but with aura and patina.

Night watchman, Ribe, Denmark.
Photo: Visit Denmark.

Photo: Nagore Uresandi

WHAT DO WE MEAN BY SUSTAINABILITY?

by Dr. Nagore Uresandi Espinosa, Director and Founder at IN2DESTINATION research and consultancy in tourism (www.in2destination.com)

Is every single person that fits the definition of a visitor a sustainability and climate change conscious person who acts accordingly when they travel? Clearly not. Depending on what we understand by conscious, it goes from 62% to 28% of global visitors. Are there visitors this conscious that find it difficult to discover sustainable choices when they travel? Definitively! Hence, let's be transparent, clear and straightforward about how amazing a place is to experience without necessarily using the word 'sustainable'. Don't worry, the search engine algorithm will still include your offering in the search results!

Many destinations and tourism companies across the globe have a climate change and sustainability mindset. The experiences they offer to visitors include many details that are thought through to minimise negative impact and maximise positive impact. However, they are not shining when it comes to communicating 'why do we do what we do' so that the discerning visitor connects with them. What does this mean? Instead of saying, 'Check out our sustainable wine tasting', say: 'Have you considered what happens with the waste we generate when we enjoy a wine tasting? In our vineyard we...' and 'To apply circular economy to our waste, we invite you to be part of it!'

Many destinations and tourism companies across the globe have a climate change and sustainability mindset. The experiences they offer to visitors include many details that are thought through to minimise negative impact and maximise positive impact.

THE OD ARTS FESTIVAL by Simon Lee Dicker, Co-Founder and Director, OSR Projects (www.odartsfestival.co.uk; www.osrprojects.co.uk)

In May 2025, OSR Projects will hold the fourth edition of its biennial three-day Od Arts Festival, named after the crooked stream that weaves its way between the two historic villages of East and West Coker.

This contemporary arts festival has, since its inauguration in 2018, disrupted the surface stillness of its rural setting. The theme this year is 'Thinking in Circles', with 20 new commissions and recent works by 18 artists and a collective exploring cycles of growth, production and consumption in rural Somerset. The art works, involving different media, will appear in locations across the two villages – including Dawe's Twineworks, the Great Hall in Coker Court, St Michaels Church, the cemetery chapel, village hall and in a former car dealership. The festival invites participants (residents and visitors) to consume new ways of thinking, sharing food and drink, laughs and ideas, and to grow together.

It is typical of the innovative and experiential community-focused work of OSR Projects since it set down its roots in West Coker's Old School Room in 2011.

Andy Parker's installation at Dawe's Twineworks, The Od Arts Festival. OSR Projects.

UP NORWAY by Torunn Tronsvang, Founder and CXO (www.upnorway.com)

At Up Norway, we strive to create enriching journeys that immerse guests in the culture, history and traditions of a place, but the essence of travel really lies in authentic human connections in the destination. Norway's soul is found in its people, landscapes and flavours, which is why our Culinary Journey is so special. From foraging with local chefs to dining in hidden fjord-side gems, we curate experiences that allow travellers to taste, feel and understand Norway in a deeply personal way. We encourage travellers to slow down, appreciate each moment and discover the destination through its stories.

Right: Ålesund Open Air Museum, Norway.
Photo: Terry Stevens.

HOW TO TRAVEL by The School of Life (www.theschooloflife.com)

The 2018 pocket manual *How To Travel* presents a template for a fresh way to experience destinations: drawing rather than taking pictures, cherishing memories, going for a walk, longing to talk to strangers.

It advocates we should dare to fully savour the modest pleasures offered to us; walk ever so slowly, as you will see it no better for going fast; follow a path and wander freely through the neglected regions of your inner landscape.

Left: 'What the Butler Saw', a 1950s arcade machine, National History Museum, St. Fagans, Cardiff. Photo: Terry Stevens.

CREATING MEMORABLE GOOD HIGHLAND FOOD EXPERIENCES
by Yvonne and Mike Crook, Founders of Good Highland Food (www.goodhighlandfood.com)

Nestled in the heart of the Scottish Highlands, this award-winning husband and wife are founders of Good Highland Food, which has redefined event catering through a passionate commitment to local produce and genuine Highland hospitality.

The company encapsulates the essence of the Highlands, where breathtaking landscapes and rich cultural history converge. Their approach is deeply rooted in their own Highland heritage. They emphasise the importance of local produce, carefully sourced from producers, often families in communities each with their own rich food heritage. Every ingredient tells a story, whether it's the fresh fish from the ocean or lochs or fast-flowing rivers, the delectable game from local estates or artisanal cheeses.

By highlighting the product's connections with the people and the place, GHF is able to serve exceptional dishes, strengthen community bonds and celebrate the essence of the local terroir. This deep appreciation for the Highlands shines through every plate, transforming meals into deep experiences steeped in tradition. From festivals and family gatherings in Scottish castles to remote bothies, visitors are directly connected to the Highlands. The mission of GHF is simple: through a commitment to marrying local produce with sophisticated preparation and presentation, it is possible to enrich the spirit of Highland hospitality, thus taking the guests on a journey, with every bite embracing the stories and flavours that define this special place.

Photo: Good Highland Food.

THE SUBTLE, NOT THE SPECTACULAR by Peter Zöch, Snøhetta, Innsbruck, Austria (www.snohetta.com)

Landscapes hold wondrous power. They connect human and non-human worlds; they can comfort or confront, inspire or frighten. Landscapes are simultaneously young and ancient; they will always exist and continue to change regardless of design or intervention. Yet, while landscapes can be shaped by an accumulation of forces and time, they can be imagined through image, text and storytelling.

With practice, landscapes can be 'read', often revealing languages, idioms and dialects unique to the specific context of time and space. Like storytelling, landscapes can tell the stories of past and present, of cause and effect, of people and culture. The simple notion of a 'path' can offer an immersive journey through place and time.

At Innsbruck's Nordkette mountain range, the Path of Perspectives introduces a select sequence of moments. The mountain path is an invitation for visitors to read and experience the alpine landscape. We were asked to design a spectacular intervention, a sensation for visitors, but we are convinced that the alpine landscape offers plenty of sensations. The subtle design interventions give the visitor hints on how to read the landscape. The act of reading is supported by quotes from Ludwig Wittgenstein inscribed in the architectural elements. In his *Philosophical Investigations,* the philosopher reflects on the difficulties of seeing a landscape. 'In his discussion of seeing he emphasizes the enormous ambiguity of what is in our visual field and the way that we need to be trained to see', Wittgenstein scholar Allan Janik comments. His selection of Wittgenstein thoughts on seeing and thinking gives a dual meaning to the Path of Perspectives. Visitors are not only invited to 'read' the landscape but to take a moment to reflect, both inwardly and out over the landscape, emphasising the ambiguity of the trail.

As with all our projects, our design interventions are a reaction to the place and its context. We begin by questioning assumptions and by considering the context of environmental, cultural and historical conditions of the sites and the people we engage. Our design interventions weave unique contexts in with conceptual thinking.

The path itself might be read as a mere infrastructural intervention, or as an intellectual confrontation. Modest design gestures may unfold spectacular stories, or only entice visitors to take a stroll and offer a place to rest. The ingredients are obvious, the outcome is defined by the users and observers. They might experience a place of wonder.

UNDERSTANDING THE PLACE AND PEOPLE by Sammy Leslie (Owner, Castle Leslie and Castle Leslie Foundation) and Brian Baldwin (CEO, Castle Leslie) (www.castleleslie.com)

Understanding Place – Setting the Scene

We live on a shared planet. Our world just seems faster, more cluttered and ever more disconnected from the natural world. We evolved over millions of years in tandem with Mother Earth, yet in a very short time we found oil and lost our way. Reconnecting with the planet we call home is more important than ever, and travel is often the way we seek to do so. For us, in this special corner of Ireland, it is about truly understanding what we have, the many layers built up over the last 10,000 years or so, since the vast ice sheets created our landscape of loughs and drumlins. Through genuine curiosity about place and people, we aim to create truly, madly, deeply authentic experiences that listen to the heartbeat of the land, the whispering of the winds and the voices of the many generations, travel experiences that are both calming and playful, sleepy and soulful, places to connect with the natural world and to spark deeper connections with each other.

Understanding People – Happy Teams Make Happy Experiences

Castle Leslie Estate is a working example of sustainable tourism through its measures to protect, restore and safeguard the built heritage and natural assets for future generations. For centuries, the Leslie family have sought to improve this place, creating a haven for people and nature by enhancing the environment and wildlife within the estate's walls.

It is our hope that our guests' experiences will allow them to reconnect with nature and to find a refuge from the outside world, surrounded by ancient forests, rolling hills and peaceful waters; a tranquil, timeless atmosphere, wonderful staff, exceptional food and discernible charm. We invite visitors to step away from the hustle and bustle of life and we hope they leave here relaxed, rejuvenated and with a better understanding of the importance of the survival of this historical estate. At the heart of delivering this purpose, mission and vision are the people – our team – who strive to create an environment where everyone feels valued, celebrated for their uniqueness and empowered to give their best.

Photo: Castle Leslie.

I FEEL SLOVENIA

SLOVENIA. MY WAY OF ESCAPE.

#ifeelsLOVEnia
#myway

SLOVENIA UNIQUE EXPERIENCES
Recommended by Slovenian Tourist Board

www.slovenia.info

KITZBÜHEL

THE MOST LEGENDARY SPORTS TOWN IN THE ALPS

WWW.KITZBUEHEL.COM

7. BE INSPIRED BY THESE WORDS

Frank Zappa (1940–1993)
'The mind is like a parachute: it only works when it is open.'

Edward Abbey (1927–1989)
'Walking makes the world much bigger and thus more interesting. You have time to observe the details.'

Robert Gover (1958–)
'Admired communities create amazing, imaginative stuff that people dream and talk about.'

John Muir (1838–1914)
'Went for a walk, one morning and being out, resolved to stay all day, for being out I found, was really going in.'

Freeman Tilden (1883–1980)
'Put there just a spark – ignite curiosity.'

William Dampier (1651–1715)
'A lack of prejudice and an inextinguishable curiosity makes one an instinctive traveller.'

Ralph Waldo Emerson (1803–1882)
'Nothing can bring you happiness but yourself, especially how you choose to think about your situation.'

Frederick Law Olmsted (1822–1903)
'The possession of knowledge does not kill the sense of wonder and mystery. There will always be mystery.'

Maya Angelou (1928–2014)
'People never forget how you make them feel.'

Rachel Carson (1907–1964)
'A sense of wonder. I would ask that a gift to each child in the world be a sense of wonder so indestructible it would last throughout life, as an unfailing antidote against boredom and disenchantments of later years.'

The Oslo Open Air Museum, Norway.
Photo: Terry Stevens.

8. OUR CURATED COLLECTION OF GREAT EXPERIENCES

The Twist is a gallery, a bridge and a sculpture all in one.

Photo: Visit Norway

WE HAVE NOT USED AN OBJECTIVE SCIENTIFIC MODEL TO MAKE THIS SELECTION.

They are experiences that we regard as being exceptional on many levels. They meet our criteria for creating a spark and nurturing ideas of a sense of place. They all adhere to dimensions of psychogeography. They all generate deep emotional responses amongst participants. They all involve the host community. They inspire.

They make visitors stay longer, helping to develop a connection with the destination and emerging with a better understanding and appreciation of the people, culture, heritage, language and landscape of the place they have visited. Intuitively, we knew these are great experiences before we experienced them all for ourselves – the ultimate test. We present them in no particular order. They are all winners.

Photos: Terry Stevens.

CAP A MAR, BARCELONA, CATALUNYA
(www.capamarbcn.com; www.facebook.com/capamarbcn)

The organisation was born in a fisherman's family of la Barceloneta. As heirs of that tradition, this generation wants to preserve and celebrate the cultural heritage of the fisherman's job, the traditions of the harbour of la Barceloneta and demonstrate sustainable fishing ideas. The aim, through a range of customised experiences, is to make the citizens feel like it is theirs and, together with visitors, share its values and appreciate the life, work and knowledge of the fishermen.

Fishing family. Challenges perceptions. Sustainable fishing. Honest. Wandering. Juxtaposed old Barcelona, new marina. Explores conflicts. Globally relevant. Hands on. Passion. Emotional. Real people. Discursive. All the senses. Provocative.

Cap A Mar Tour. Photo: NJOY Catalonia.

Cap A Mar. Photo: NJOY Catalonia.

The Spark and a Sense of Wonder

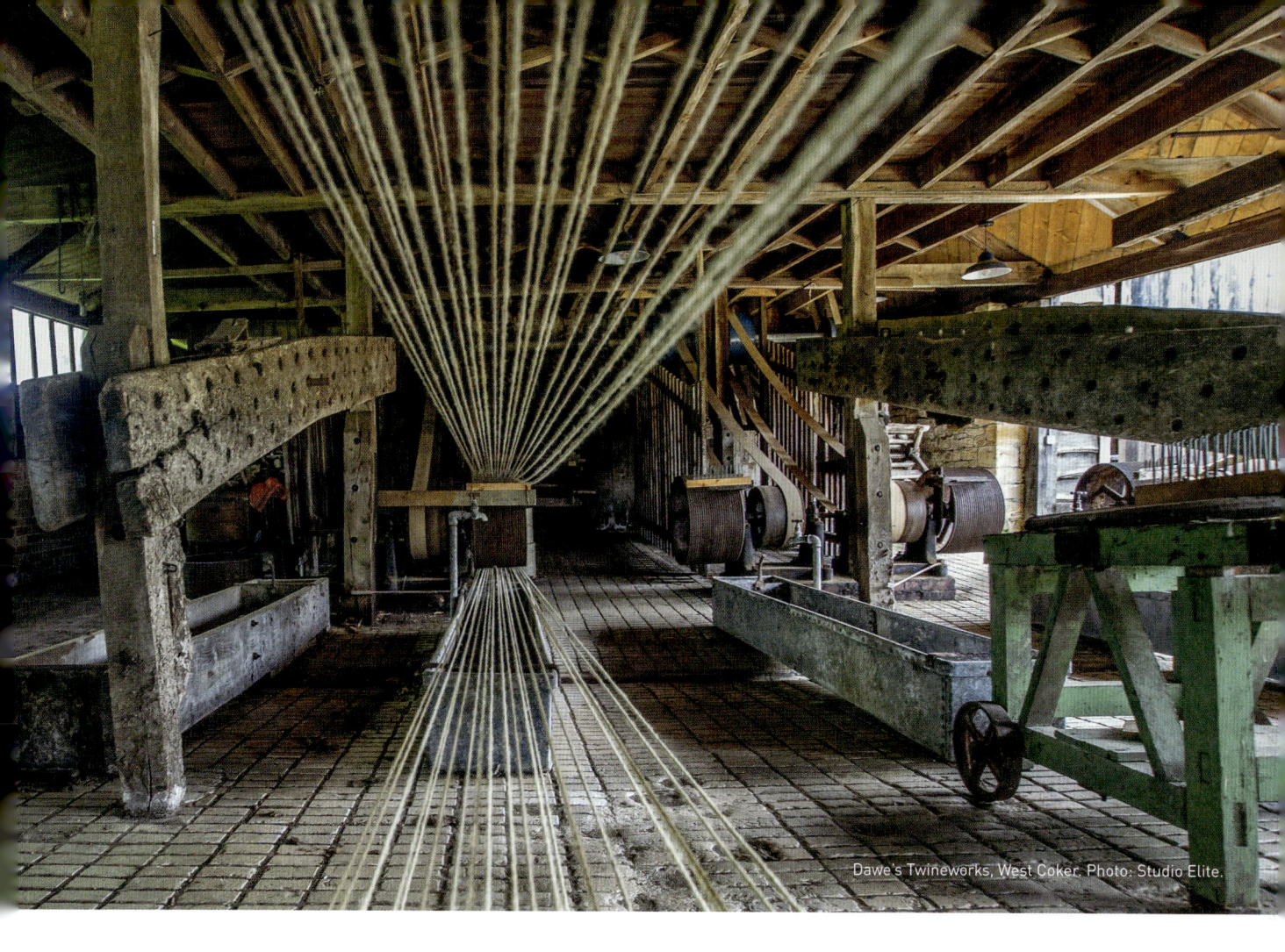

Dawe's Twineworks, West Coker. Photo: Studio Elite.

DAWES TWINEWORKS, WEST COKER, ENGLAND
(www.facebook.com/dawestwineworks)

This restored twineworks in the Somerset village of West Coker is the only working Victorian factory of its type in England. It is the emblematic and iconic feature for the communities of East, North and West Coker to share the story of Coker Canvas – the best sailcloth in the world for 300 years. The twineworks hosts the Od Festival, open days, live music and theatre as well as visitors meeting local volunteers.

The twineworks allows visitors to touch, smell, hear, taste and become fully immersed in this inspiring project. Its unique story is told in the book *Bucked in the Yarn* which won the Alan Ball Award for the best local history book in the UK in 2024.

Real local people. Revealing. Restored. Loved. Passion. Respected. Understated. Endearing human stories. Modest. Innovative. Multi-layered. Alive. Colourful. Surprising. Extraordinary achievements. Hard graft. Globally significant impact.

Scale. Year-round. Free-flow. Changing perspectives. Community initiative. Bold. Creative. Enthusiastic. Redistribute tourists. All weather. Self-managed. Industrial setting. Disruptive. Antidote to formal galleries. Evolution of 2009 European Capital of Culture. Accessible.

Photo: Terry Stevens.

THE MURAL HARBOUR, LINZ, AUSTRIA
(muralharbor.at; www.linztourismus.at)

A number of European cities (Ljubljana, Vienna and Berlin) celebrate their vibrant street art culture with free-form outdoor graffiti galleries and tours. Vienna has welcomed Dutch artist Judith De Leeuw's enormous artworks featuring universal themes of grief and happiness. One of the most coordinated and impressive street art experiences of urban art is the 135ha Mural Harbour in the reimagined industrial city of Linz. The outdoor gallery has more than 300 graffiti artworks by artists from over 40 countries, including Aryz, Lors, Nychos and Roa. Established in 2014, based on the desire by workers and residents to 'pimp up the area', the mission is to draw visitors to this part of the city by presenting a spectrum of urban art in an oversized format, challenging the visitor to take a different perspective on the setting. The gallery, set amongst cranes, warehouses and shipyards, has no opening hours. You can visit by boat from the Danube or on foot with an artist and do a crash course in graffiti art.

THE COMEDY CARPET, BLACKPOOL, ENGLAND
(www.gordonyoung.info)

This is public art on steroids. It is an extraordinary celebration of British comedy and sense of humour located on the promenade of this traditional seaside resort in the shadow of the famous Blackpool Tower and theatre.

Every step on this iconic 2,200m² horizontal sculpture makes you laugh aloud with the best jokes, catchphrases and songs of 1,000 artists who have performed in the theatre, told with 160,000 granite letters set in a special form of concrete. The Comedy Carpet, created by artist Gordon Young in collaboration with designers Why Not Associates, triggers many happy memories and has been appropriated by the Alzheimer's Society.

Passion. Clever. Sense of place. Scale. Innovative. Year-round. Free access. Humour. Breaks rules. All weather. Must visit. Sensory. Engaging. Immersive. Relevant to setting. Value for money. Enhances destination.

Photos: Gordon Young.

THE PATH OF PERSPECTIVES BY SNØHETTA, INNSBRUCK, AUSTRIA (www.snohetta.com)

Located on Innsbruck's Nordkette mountain and designed by Snøhetta for the Nordkettenbahn Cable Car Company, this project elevates a simple footpath offering wonderful panoramic views of the surrounding Karwendel alpine landscape into a journey of wonderment and inspiration.

Along a meandering 2.8km hiking trail is a series of ten architectural interventions (viewpoints and benches). Each makes a unique statement as they appear to emerge from the terrain. They invite the trail users to stop, contemplate the view and ask questions about the environment and their place within the natural setting. Quotes from the Austrian philosopher Ludwig Wittgenstein (born in Vienna, schooled in Linz) are inscribed on the installations.

The quotes further invite the visitor to reflect, both inwardly and out over the landscape, giving dual meaning to the path of perspectives.

Free. Challenging perspectives. Art meets nature. Innovative. Clever. Year-round. All weather. Passion. Philosophy. Profound. Added value. Recreation. Bold. Creative.

Path of Perspectives, Innsbruck, Snøhetta. Photo: Christian Flatscher.

Multi-layered. Bookable. Value added. Heritage. Gastronomy. Community. Real. Authentic. Challenging story. Occasionally available. Immersive. Customised. Curated.

MYSTERIES OF THE SUBMERGED VILLAGES, THE ŠALEŠKA VALLEY, SLOVENIA (www.slovenia.info)

An inspiring story of how an experience can transform the face of a destination. Underground in the Šaleška Valley lies Slovenia's largest coal deposit. More than 230 million tonnes of coal have been mined in this area over almost 150 years. Mining has left a lasting mark on the valley and its people. Where once there were villages, today there are lakes. What has happened to the houses, the schools, the churches? Why did they sink, and where did the villagers go? Discover the incredible life stories of the villagers, the miners, the people of Velenje, told by the grandson of a miner. Take the elevator down into the tunnels 160 metres underground and experience the everyday life of a miner. Take a boat across the surface of Velenje Lake and take a virtual plunge into the depths that still hold the treasures of a mining family. Enjoy a selection of local delicacies at the lookout point. Take away an unforgettable experience and a special symbol of the Velenje miners.

THE MAGNIFICENT SEVEN: INSPIRING STORIES OF POSAVJE CASTLES, SLOVENIA (www.slovenia.info)

Connecting multiple destinations and individual attractions into a cohesive, authentic story, this is a whole day of wandering and discovering the exciting castle stories and legends from the past, taking visitors back to the times of powerful noble families and their destinies. A carefully interwoven and coordinated learning experience about cultural heritage and authentic local specialities promises an unforgettable day. The experience includes top-class 'castle' cuisine by the best Posavje chefs, who specialise in dishes prepared with local, authentic ingredients, along with the best Posavje wines. Visitors will also experience chocolate making, an authentic blacksmith's workshop and other castle surprises. The route includes the seven castles of Posavje: Brežice, Kunšperk, Mokrice, Rajhenburg, Sevnica and Svibno as well as the former Cistercian monastery Kostanjevica na Krki.

Photo: Slovenia Tourist Board.

Heritage. Whole day. Wandering. Gastronomy. Culture. Architecture. Small group or individuals. Customised. Bookable. Value added. Multi-layered. Expert knowledge.

The Spark and a Sense of Wonder

MASTER PLEČNIK, LJUBLJANA, SLOVENIA
(www.slovenia.info)

An experience that enriches and enhances UNESCO cultural heritage, this is an intimate journey in the footsteps of the visionary master architect Jože Plečnik and his great mind, getting to know Plečnik's legacy through an experience puzzle for a small group. Embark on a well-rounded trip that follows the trail of Plečnik's plans and visions for the city and get a special insight into his achievements and countless interesting architectural details. The trip takes you along the trail of Plečnik's plans and visions, both on land and on the river. On foot and with a storyteller, you will discover piece by piece one of Europe's greatest architects of the 20th century, who provided Ljubljana with its eternal beauty and charm. He created a land and water axis with masterpieces that are today a UNESCO World Heritage Site.

The experience includes special features such as a lesson in Plečnik's cabinet, drinking the master's favourite coffee in an intimate atrium, counting original candelabras and a surprise picnic in the garden of Plečnik House.

Multi-layered. Curated. Architecture. Urban. Walking. Design. Small groups. Bookable. Year-round. Gastronomy. Immersive. Customised. Added value. Expert knowledge.

Photo: Slovenia Tourist Board.

DISCOVER THE WORLD OF THE BROWN BEAR, KOČEVJE, SLOVENIA (www.slovenia.info)

Enter the world of this formerly closed tract of land and the mysterious forests of Kočevje to explore nature in all its primal glory. This area is home to the largest brown bear population and the highest number of primeval forest remnants in Europe. Join an expedition to explore the migration paths of the brown bear. Experience the wilderness of the Kočevje forests under the experienced guidance of a local expert. Get a good close-up of the king of the Kočevje forests and taste unusual edible forest herbs. This is an experience that will change your view of the forest and wild animals that takes place in the largest uniform forest area in Europe, one of the rare places in the world where it is still possible to see three large predators in their natural habitat – the bear, wolf and lynx. Follow wild animal tracks to discover stories from the forest and learn to listen to the silence in a place that no Wi-Fi signal can reach. Learn the skills of picking edible plants and treat yourself to a lunch in the vicinity of a primeval forest.

Nature. Ancient forest.
Primal. Expedition. Adventure.
Conservation. Raw. Customised.
Expert knowledge. Emotional.
Limited access. Small group.
Bookable. Curated.

THE NEWT IN SOMERSET, ENGLAND
(www.thenewtinsomerset.com)

The Newt is exceptional. In the making for six years, it opened in August 2019 and is now really fulfilling its promise as a reimagined Somerset farm and estate. It never fails to enchant, create wonderment and pose deep questions about sustainable land management. It is impossible to categorise or define. It has a boutique accommodation, extraordinary gardens, woodland and tree-top walks, a reconstructed Roman villa, a cydery, expositions on gardening and perfected home-grown produce. Along with its sibling project of Babylonstoren (Western Cape), The Newt is a hybrid solution to meeting the many varied needs of contemporary tourists. The key to its success is the vision of the owners, South African Koos Bekker and his wife Karen Roos, of whom it was once said that they prefer to share their creation rather than boast about it. A deep understanding of what makes a great experience underpinned with scholarship, authenticity, bright, engaging hosts and money-no-object attention to detail makes this a new benchmark in the way we consider the environment of hospitality at scale.

Hybrid. Creative. Multi-layered. Charging. Accommodation. Day visits. Year-round. All-weather. Re-imaging. Sustainability. Scales. Varied. Diverse. Capitally intensive. Rural. Estate management. Immersive. People.

The Newt in Somerset. Photo: Terry Stevens.

Turku Cathedral. Photo: Visit Turku.

TURKU AND THE DOERZ, FINLAND
(www.visitturku.fi)

Turku Touring Oy is the not-for-profit destination management organisation for this former capital of Finland and gateway to the Finnish south-west archipelago. The company excels in innovation and encouraging others in curating creative experiences. One such initiative is the Doerz of Turku – a platform and community that links travellers to locals to find authentic real-life experiences in the region. Founded by Tomi Virtanen and Arte Aaltonen, Doerz has pioneered the 'like a local' concept in Finland's Christmas City and the European Capital of Culture (2011). There is cherry picking with Marjetta, flea market shopping with Ida and beer tasting with Tapani – over 50 local people are now involved as freelancers.

Local people. Real life. Innovative. Passion. Sharing. Off the beaten track. Scalable. Multiple options. Exploration. Customised. Tradition. Hobbies. Discovery. Dark stories. Light stories. Individuals. Small groups. Year-round.

SUMMER OF LOVE EXPERIENCES, SAN FRANCISCO, USA
(www.sftravel.com; www.nationalgeographic.com)

San Francisco, and especially the neighbourhood of Haight-Ashbury, became the epicentre of the hippie culture, which started in 1964 as a utopian ideal of peace, love and flower children.

However, with its heyday in the summer of 1967 (captured in Scott McKenzie's hit record 'San Francisco (Be Sure to Wear Some Flowers in Your Hair)', the dream was virtually over by 1968 when the streets filled to capacity and the trip turned bad, man. Today, there are multiple and varied opportunities to get close to this story by wandering in the footsteps of Janis Joplin and the Grateful Dead and exploring the key sites, such as Hippie Hill and the City Lights bookstore (founded in 1953 by poet Lawrence Ferlinghetti and Peter D. Martin) – the alternative culture's 'Literary Landmark'.

Multi-layered. Immersive. Art. Architecture, Fashion. Music. Urban. Flexible. Year-round. All weather. Free or bookable. Walking. Counter-culture. Poetry. Creative.

Photo: Terry Stevens.

VIENNA ALTERNATIVE WALKING EXPERIENCES
(www.wein.info; www.viennawurstelstand.com)

Alternative? In Vienna? Yes. In 1857, Emperor Franz Joseph demolished the medieval walls of the capital to link the city with the suburbs. This was the start of Vienna in the new age. Today, the writer Becki Enright explains that 'history is re-imagined in the creative spaces between the ancient avenues intertwined with artistic rebellion.' The alternative Vienna is best explored on foot (like most of the former Hapsburg cities).

Explore Zollergasse and Kirchengasse bars, discover street art or visit the Ankerbrotfabrik or The Werk, counter-cultural hotspots in the 10th district that sit alongside that district's community buildings. Walk with a homeless person. Get the Vienna hiking guide and passport then follow the Wiener Weinwandertag trail through urban vineyards in Heurigenpfas.

Alternative. Walking. Multi-layered. Art. Architecture. Gastronomy. Urban and rural. Flexible. Free. All weather. Year-round. Community. Dispersal. Discovery. Explore.

Photo: Visit Austria.

Community. Regeneration. Renewal. Changing perceptions. Creative. Local. Scale. Free. Accessible. Year-round. All weather. Architecture. Art. Bold. Culture. Villages. Countryside. Multi-layered.

Photo: Visit Vorarlberg.

VILLAGE STROLLS WHERE TRADITION MEETS MODERNITY
IN BREGENZERWALD, VORARLBERG, AUSTRIA
(www.bregenzerwald.at; www.vorarlberg.travel)

What are the origins of Bregenzerwald's unique look and feel? Which values and ideas have helped to shape this rural area, sandwiched between Germany, Switzerland and Liechtenstein in western Austria? What qualities and characteristics might attentive visitors notice in the villages and surrounding nature? 'Umgang Bregenzerwald' is a series of 12 short paths through the villages that attempt to provide answers to these questions. Visitors can immerse themselves in this unique environment and discover how people interact with their surroundings, the landscape, regional products, their homes, their culture and with other people and themselves. This is the idea behind the 'Umgang Bregenzerwald' (village walks). Approximately 30,000 people live in the 23 villages within the valley community of Vorarlberg, an area known for preserving tradition yet being surprisingly open to new ideas. Insights into the behaviour, the 'Umgang', of the people of Bregenzerwald are illuminated along 12 circuit paths through 13 villages in the region. Wandering these trails, visitors discover selected objects, providing insight into a unique way of life that continues today and the way people in the Bregenzerwald deal with their environment.
The walks are of differing lengths as they journey through the villages of Au, Schoppernau, Mellau, Bizau, Bezau-Reuthe, Andelsbuch, Schwarzenberg, Egg, Lingenau, Langenegg, Hittisau and Krumbach, giving visitors a modern interpretation of ancient traditions.

LA MACHINE AND THE GREEN LINE, NANTES, FRANCE
(www.nantes-tourisme.com; www.levoyageanantes.fr; www.lesmachines-nantes.fr)

If ever there was a prize for the most successful, radical, canny and imaginative transformation of a post-industrial port city then Nantes would be on top of the podium. Leading the bold turnaround have been four innovative, determined personalities, supported by an army of creative talent, enlightened political leaders and an open-minded community. The four visionary cultural activists behind the reinvention of Nantes included François Delaroziere. By 2011, it had become apparent that art and tourist experiences were intimately linked and Le Voyage à Nantes was created – a merger of the cultural bodies and the tourism office. Its first initiative took the city by surprise. One morning, residents woke to find a 15km pink line (now green) painted on the city streets – a simple tool for people to follow to explore the city. Then came Les Machines de L' Île – Nantes. Amazing in every sense, this was the novel response of the desire to alter the perceptions of the city by harnessing the collective imagination of the citizens to generate ideas to create extraordinary experiences across the city. The signature features are the fantastical mechanical monsters created by Les, best exemplified by Le Grand Elephant – a 50-tonne mechanical beast that strides around the L' Île de Nantes roaring and spraying water – and Le Carrousel des Mondes Marins.

Creative. Art meets engineering. Bold. Community. Accessible. Scale. Profound. Regeneration. Changing perceptions. Year-round. All weather. Iconic. Symbolic. Multi-disciplinary.

TERAN WINE AND WALK, MOTOVUN, ISTRIA, CROATIA
(www.istra.hr; www.hr.roxanich.com)

Now in its seventh edition, this is one of the most talked about and appealing adventure walks. Held annually in September, this 12km walk weaves its way through the changing colours of the vineyards around the hilltop village of Motovun, often using the Parenzana Trail, which is the track of an old railway. The walk combines wine tasting with gastronomy, recreation facilitating the meeting of friends and strangers alike. En route there are eight wineries providing tasting stations where up to 700 walkers meet with the winemakers, local producers and chefs. Organised by the local community, the walk starts and finishes at the extraordinary family-owned and run Roxanich Winery and Design Hotel. This inland experience is matched by its sister event, the Wine Walk by the Sea, based in Novigrad.

Multilayered. Annual. Bookable. Gastronomy. Landscape. Walking. Talking. Passion. Extends the tourist year. Rural. Relaxed. Passion. Exercise. Socialising. Community meets tourist. Countryside. Coast. Traditional. Culture. Immersive.

Wine Walk, Istria. Photo: Visit Istria.

THE BRYNE HAALAND EXPERIENCE, BRYNE, NORWAY
(www.visitnorway.com)

With a very tongue-in-cheek promotion that begins 'Yes, we love Haaland!', the small town of Bryne in Jæren – a town of 12,500 inhabitants in southwestern Norway and home of one of the biggest football players of our time, the Norwegian 'Viking' Erling Braut Haaland – has created the Haaland Experience. Celebrating the hometown of one of the greatest living players in the world, the experience includes: take a selfie in front of the two street art images of Haaland, one by Anette Moi and the other one by Pøbel; visit Bryne Stadion, the home pitch of Erling's first club, Bryne FK; taste Bryne's speciality: Farse at Pylsebuå te Håland (Håland's hot dog stand); dine at the Chinese restaurant Wen Hua House, where Haaland used to eat; stop by Hole Gard at Voll or Jerseymeieriet at Herikstad to get a taste of Haaland's 'magic potion', fresh cow's milk.

Community. Year-round. Multi-layered. Free. Accessible. Food. Football. Art. Contemporary culture. Creative. Humour. Local. Immersive.

Photo: Visit Norway.

Ivan Vidmar. Photo: Terry Stevens.

Photo: San Servolo.

SAN SERVOLO BREWERY, BUJE, ISTRIA, CROATIA (www.sanservolo.beer)

Established in 2012, the Brewery Bujska Pivoaranow has a new facility that opened to visitors in 2024.
It is set in an unprepossessing industrial unit on the fringe of the historic hilltop village of Buje (known as the 'sentinel of Istria'), located 10km inland from the Adriatic Sea. This artisan-made unfiltered beer uses the crystal-clear water from the spring of St. Ivan as a key ingredient. The brewery is the vision of brothers Simon and Goran Grbac, whose aim is to link the traditions, heritage and gastronomy of Buje with an innovative approach to telling its story to visitors. The gourmet enjoyment and the promise of a story in every bottle is delivered by the aptly named beer sommelier, Ivan Vidmar. He is the 'curator of taste' – a storyteller with every sip. Humour, art, culture, real insight and highly customised experiences give this brewery a preeminent status in its genre.

Relaxed. Real. Authentic. Artisan. Gastronomy. Culture. Heritage. Multilayered. Multilingual. Customised. Passion. Year-round. All weather. Tradition. Excellence. Knowledge. Art. Great beer. All senses. Private investment. Community involvement.

THE MURAL & POLITICAL TOURS, WEST BELFAST, NORTHERN IRELAND
(www.visitwestbelfast.com)

Fáilte Feirste Thiar/Visit West Belfast have taken the lead in supporting West Belfast-based Coiste Irish Political Tours (www.coiste.ie) and Taxi Trax (www.taxitrax.com) in a wide range of experiences, engaging visitors with first-hand narratives across Belfast communities. The Joint Falls/Shankill Tour offered by Coiste blends the narratives of local Republican former prisoners with former Loyalist activists in their localities. The Falls Mural walking tour and 'the Black Taxi' tours involve activists and former political prisoners, providing a deep insight into the most recent phase of the Anglo-Irish conflict from their very personal perspectives as they visit the many and varied sites where the murals reveal both the local and wider history of Ireland. A more recent addition to the collection of murals is one dedicated to Patrick O'Connell, known in Spain (especially in Catalunya) as Don Patricio, the man who saved Barcelona Football Club. During the annual Féile an Phobail (see page 71), additional specialist tours are available, such as Tom Hartley's (former Lord Mayor of Belfast) walking tour of the Belfast Cemetery and the traditional music tour.

Community. Heritage. Culture. Creative. Outdoors. Urban. Walking. Tour or free-flow. Chargeable or free. Year-round. All weather. Authentic. Challenging. Emotional. Passion.

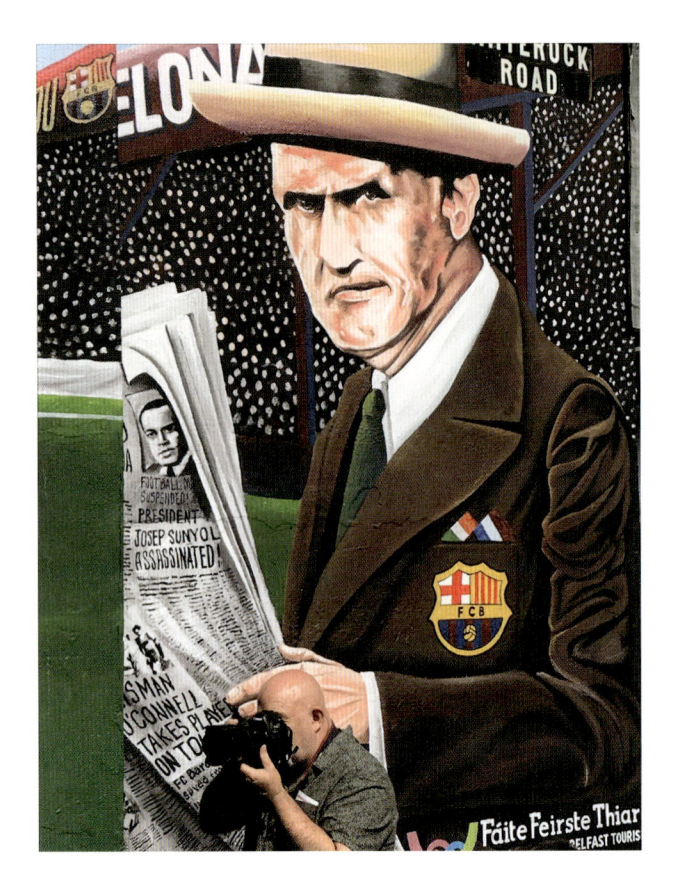

Top: Patrick O'Connell Mural.
Photo: Terry Stevens.

Above: The Bobby Sands Mural.
Photo: Coiste and Visit West Belfast.

MAR DE MALVASIA EXPERIENCE BY THE RANXO MARINER FISHERMEN, SITGES, CATALONIA (www.museusdesitges.cat)

This is one of a large number of initiatives contributing to Catalonia's status as 2025 World Region of Gastronomy. The Mariner Ranches (Ranxo) of Sitges is the oldest of the Catalan fishermen's guilds. It is exclusively based on traditional artisanal methods catching fish using age-old methods such as pole, long-line, tremall and, for shellfish, cages. On Fridays, visitors can arrange to meet some of the local fishermen and their families at the Guild's building, the Confraria de Pesca Artesanal de Sitges, where they chat about the fishing traditions, share stories about their lives, their concerns about the conservation of the seas followed by the fishermen cooking a shared meal based on their catch of the day.

Community. Sharing. Tradition. Culture, Artisan craft. Environmental conservation, Authentic. Real. Heritage. Gastronomy. Passion. Customised. Honest. Relaxed. Storytelling. Interaction.

The fresh food from the seas. Photo: NJOY Catalonia.

St Michael's and All Angels Parish Church, East Coker. Photo: Studio Elite.

THE EAST COKER MARITIME AND MONARCH'S WAY WALK, EAST COKER, SOMERSET, ENGLAND (www.eastcokerparishcouncil.com)

There can be few places where you can wander around an ancient, pretty village and find the final resting place of a winner of the Nobel Prize in Literature (T. S. Eliot, 1888–1965), the birthplace of one of the world's greatest buccaneers, explorers and naturalists (William Dampier, 1651–1715), a memorial to the Great Plague, 500-year-old alms houses built on the earnings from the slave trade, a Roman villa and the former mills and weavers' cottages associated with the making of the best sailcloth in the world for 300 years – Coker Canvas. The village of East Coker is 30km from the sea, yet the community has prepared a walk for visitors to explore this maritime heritage.

In part, the trail follows the Monarch's Way, a walk that traces the route taken by King Charles II (a monarch with a dubious moral compass) on his escape from England in 1651 following defeat in the Battle of Worcester.

Community. Walking. Heritage. History. Village. Countryside. Meet local people. Poetry. Maritime. Four Quartets. Coker Canvas. Global meets local. Recreations. Passion. Real. Storytelling. Year-round. Free.

THE RODDY MCCORLEY REPUBLICAN HERITAGE CENTRE, WEST BELFAST, NORTHERN IRELAND (www.roddymccorley.com)

This is the only example in this collection focused upon a single building. It is the hub for a wide range of rare, interconnected experiences, with its community at its heart. Located in parkland in West Belfast at the foot of the Belfast Hills, the Roddy McCorley Republican Heritage Centre comprises a world-class museum, functions and events space and a contemporary modern restaurant with a rooftop terrace commanding panoramic views across Belfast. Here the guest can engage in a wide range of experiences – from playing snooker with locals, sharing stories over a beer, live music, or having a go at hurling. It is an eclectic, exceptional meeting point, offering the visitor the chance to immerse themselves in the rich history and traditions of Ireland – focusing upon the story of 200 years of Irish Republicanism told through the prism of a unique collection of locally gathered and curated historical artefacts.

Community. Culture. Heritage. Food and drink. Events. Exhibitions. Sport. Relaxed. Real. Multi-layered. People. Free. Accessible. Perspectives. Dispersal. Challenging. Storied. Stories. Emotional.

Attempting hurling. Photo: Terry Stevens.

Photo: Fáilte Feirste Thiar/Visit West Belfast.

LA BATANA AND THE ECO-MUSEUM, ROVINJ, ISTRIA, CROATIA
(www.batana.org)

This is a unique community initiative, recognised by UNESCO, which commenced in 2004. It is dedicated to a traditional, highly symbolic, small wooden boat that is the tangible expression of renewal and regeneration following the turmoil of the Yugoslavian Wars during the 1990s. The multidisciplinary project 'Batana of Rovinj – Rovigno' – a picturesque heritage town of 13,000 inhabitants – is a result of the community's desire to keep its maritime traditions alive. The small, flat-bottomed batana is the traditional fishing boat of Rovinj. The project has several elements to engage the visitor: the House of Batana is a traditional quayside fisherman's cottage with exhibition and shop; the Spacio Matika is a shared space for visitors and fishermen to share food, drink and stories; Mali Škver is a small shipyard on the square where visitors can see a boat being built; the Rovinj Regatta is the annual celebration of the boat and its traditions; and there are the batana-themed routes by sea and by boat.

Tangible and intangible heritage. Maritime tradition. Stakeholder and grassroots community. Eco museum. Passion. Real. Honest. Multilayered. Immersive. Artisan. Craft. Multi-sensory. Multilingual.

Rovinj, Croatia. Photo: Shutterstock.

Photo: Sean McKernan.

FÉILE AN PHOBAIL, BELFAST, NORTHERN IRELAND
(www.feilebelfast.com)

Féile an Phobail is Ireland's biggest community arts festival and summer school. Féile provides a programme of inclusive arts, cultural and community-based activities throughout the year, with its flagship festival, the August Féile, being the highlight of Ireland's festival calendar. Established in 1988 in response to the negative images and impacts of the 'Troubles', a group of dedicated activists from West Belfast had the vision to create an organisation to develop and showcase the talents, resilience and determination of their community. Today, Féile promotes Irish and international culture through a variety of over 300 activities in 10 days in August each year, including tours, walks, family events, youth programs, Gaeilge (Irish language) events, film and theatre, international events, sports, health and wellbeing initiatives, pride events, a summer school of lectures and debates. The festival attracts over 100,000 people and takes place on and around Falls Road in Belfast. Its mission is focused on creating a platform for inclusive arts, cultural and community-based activities throughout the year. Féile an Phobail is celebrated for promoting a positive cultural and creative reputation of West Belfast, providing diverse experiences that bring people of all backgrounds together.

Community. Culture. Immersive. Multi-layered. Free and bookable. Variety. Passion. Creative. Music. Sport, Art. Heritage. Design. Debate. Discourse. Challenging perceptions. Changing behaviour. Inclusive.

Road trip. Art. Architecture. Landscape. Culture.
Changing perceptions. Multi-layered. International.
Curated. Free access. Year-round. All weather. Vistas.
International. Creative.

NORWEGIAN NATIONAL SCENIC ROUTES (NASJONALE TURISTVEGER), NORWAY (www.nasjonerturistveger.no)

Both a journey and an attraction, the Norwegian Scenic Routes, now into its 30th year, is a success story. In the early 1990s there was a widely held view in Norway that the country was struggling to compete in the international tourism markets. The idea of the National Scenic Routes was born to help address these issues whilst stimulating economic and cultural development in peripheral communities.
In 1993, the Norwegian Parliament asked the Ministry of Transport to look at the relationship between roads and tourism. A year later, work began on a pilot project that gave four routes the status of National Scenic Routes. The roads through unique and majestic scenery already existed, so it was therefore decided that architecture and art would be used to enhance the experience, based upon the unique atmosphere, environment and sense of place at every site. There are now 2,740km of National Scenic Routes, 18 in total, with 185 installations across the country. This is a transformational scheme that has positively impacted all the communities along their routes and changed the world's perception of Norway.

It challenges our perceptions of landscape and wilderness, but, in the words of Norway's modernist architect Sverre Fehn, 'architecture, if carefully considered, could serve to elevate nature without competing with it and, in so doing, become an experience in itself.'

Above: Trollstigen Viewpoint, Geiranger, Trollstein, Norway.
Photo: Terry Stevens.

72   The Spark and a Sense of Wonder

THE GRAMONA WINERY, CATALUNYA (www.gramona.com)

Located in the Alt Penedés region in Sant Sadurni d'Anoia, 40 minutes or so northwest of Barcelona, is a family-owned vineyard producing one of the world's best sparkling wines. The winery is among the features of one of the Catalan touring routes – the Penedés Wine Route. The family has been working the land since the mid-19th century. The current generations are for a sustainable and biodynamic approach to the production of high-quality sparkling wines. A new era for Gramona began in 1945 under the stewardship of Bartomeu and Josep Lluis Gramona – the visionaries who regarded themselves as 'artisans of time' – with a range of sparkling wines that are aged for 12 years or more. The estate, in the Anoia and Bitlles river basins, uses geothermal energy and recycled water and is farmed using horses. Its visitor experience engages visitors in an understanding of the vintner's deep respect for a holistic approach to land management and imbibing the long-ageing sparkling wines.

Family. Passion. Sustainability. Gastronomy. Viticulture. Rural. Emotional. Year-round. Bookable. Cultural route. Curated. Customised. Immersive. Road trip.

Photo: Gramona Winery Collection.

THE AKSLA STEPS, ÅLESUND, NORWAY
(www.visitnorway.com)

Ålesund is a charming port on the west coast of Norway, at the entrance to the Geirangerfjord. It is known for its art nouveau architectural style from the time when the town was rebuilt after a fire in 1904. When recently checking in at the eponymous Hotel 1904, I asked the receptionist where the gym was. She raised her arm and pointed a finger towards Mount Aksla (the Town Mountain) and plainly said, 'It's out there!' To reach the Aksla viewpoint, you walk the 418 steps from the Byparken – the town park created in 1858. It is a 120m vertical climb to reach the summit, with a 9% gradient. This is a stripped-back, very simple but uplifting experience and is shared by thousands, including many children. The panoramic views of Ålesund's architecture, the surrounding archipelago, the fjords and the Sunnmøre Alps are astounding. For an additional reward, enjoy a local sweet treat called *svele* in the Restaurant Fjellstua. Every town needs an Aksla!

Basic. Free. Panorama. Landscape. Raw. Wellness. Contemplation. Must visit. Must do. Rural and urban. Walking. Multi-layered. Civic pride. Iconic. Year-round.

Ålesund, Norway. Photo: Nicolai Berntsen.

ST. TOLA'S CHEESE
(www.st-tola.ie)

Located in the heart of County Clare, close to the Cliffs of Moher, St. Tola's Irish Goat Farm has been a cornerstone of Ireland's artisanal cheese industry since 1979. Renowned for its handcrafted cheeses, the farm has become a symbol of sustainability, quality and culinary excellence.

The range of St. Tola cheeses reflects the purity and freshness of the Burren's unique environment, a UNESCO Global Geopark. Spanning 65 acres, the working farm is a destination for food enthusiasts and visitors eager to learn about the intricacies of goat farming and cheesemaking. There are personal tours that provide an immersive experience into the world of artisanal cheese production and visitors have the opportunity to meet the goats, witness feeding time and gain insight into the sustainable farming methods employed on-site.

A highlight of the tour is the cheesemaking demonstration and tastings, allowing guests to sample the distinctive flavours that define the brand. The experience is brought alive by the enthusiasm of Siobhán Ní Gháirbhith and family. They are a proud member of the Burren Food Trail, Économusée, and the Burren Ecotourism Network, St. Tola exemplifies sustainable farming and traditional craftsmanship, ensuring a legacy firmly rooted in Ireland's rich culinary landscape.

Artisan. Gastronomy. Rural. Farming. Land management. Immersive. Tastings. Bookable. Year-round. Geopark.

Photo: St. Tola's Farm.

Year-round. All weather. Outdoors. Art. Creative. Rural and urban. Challenging. Emotional. Passion. Curated. Free and charging. Immersive. Multi-layered.

Louisiana, Denmark. Photo: Terry Stevens.

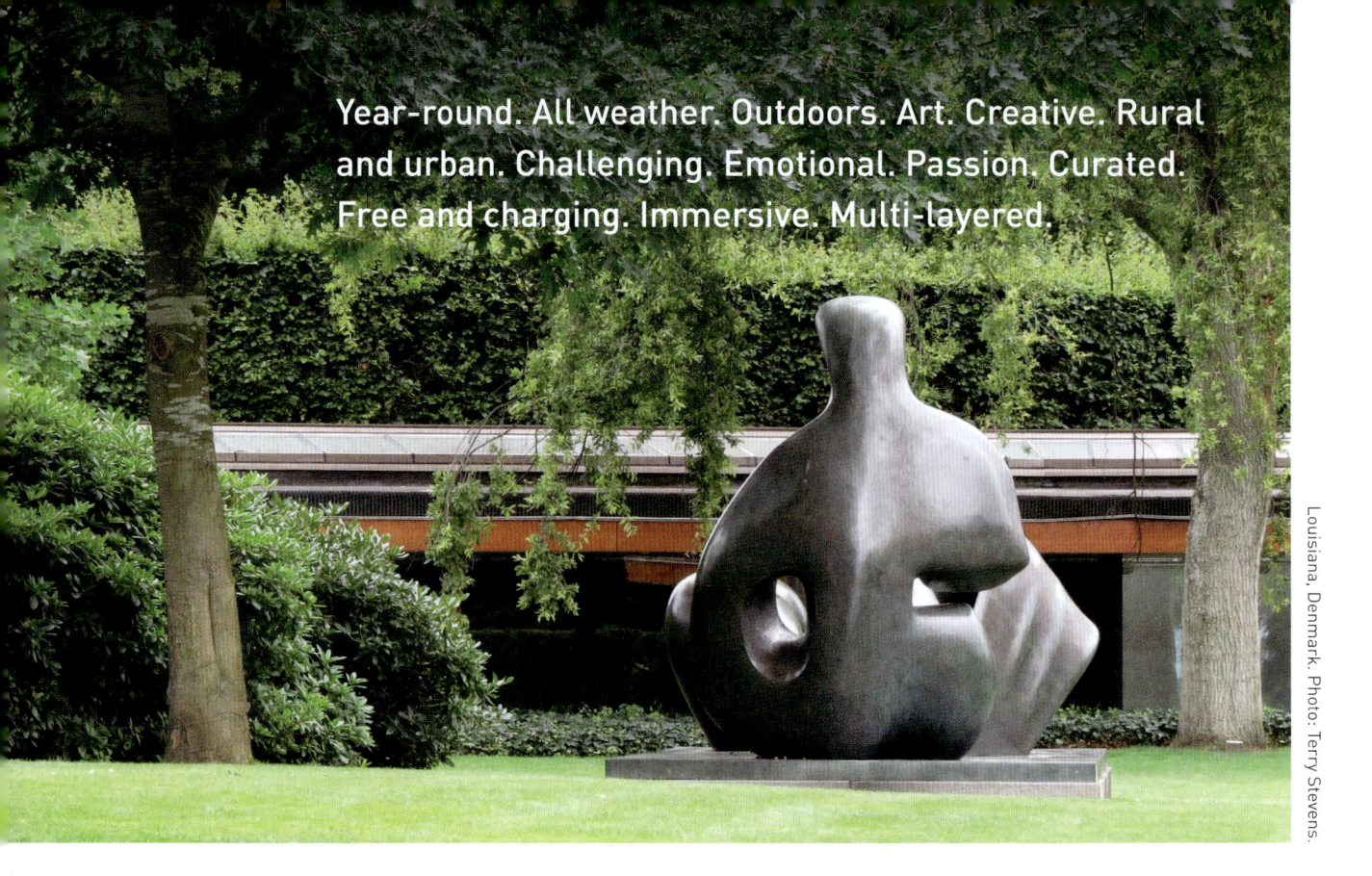

THE POWER OF SCULPTURE PARKS

In 1983 Terry Stevens developed and managed the Welsh Sculpture Trust's 'Sculpture in a Country Park' – a remarkable exhibition of 66 works by 34 internationally renowned artists, including Henry Moore, Barbara Hepworth, Elisabeth Frink, David Nash, David Kemp and Richard Deacon. The sculpture exhibition was curated by Gordon Young (see the Hall of Fame) and set in the grounds of Margam Country Park (Wales). The visitors' encounters with the artworks challenged them to ask questions about the landscape, the environment, space and their feelings, emotions and identity. In this process, the art and the artist became the midwives of psychogeography and enhanced visitor experiences. Recent research has also shown that people who regularly engage with art, such as sculpture parks, may live longer. Sculpture parks around the world have a reputation for the delivery of great experiences. Prime examples include: Yorkshire Sculpture Park (England), Storm King (USA), Jupiter Artland and the Garden of Cosmic Speculation (Scotland), Ekeberg Park (Norway), Gibbs Farm (New Zealand), Kröller-Muller (Netherlands), Louisiana (Denmark), Parikalla (Finland), Isla El Descanso (Argentina) and Valle Verzasca Footpath for Art (Switzerland).

Ekeberg Park, Oslo. Photo: Terry Stevens.

THE IMPACT OF RANDOM ACTS OF KINDNESS
(www.randomactsofkindness.org)

Many great tourist experiences happen as a result of spontaneous, unplanned encounters with strangers who perform random acts of kindness. These are acts that display care and consideration by the host to the guest – and vice versa. They are interactions that create a positive image, an atmosphere of welcome (*croeso* in Wales, *fáilte* in Ireland, ようこそ (*yōkoso*) in Japan), and can deepen a visitor's relationship with the destination in a profound way.

Repucon's Tourism Experience Pulse™ model and the impact of Turku's Doerz platform regularly highlight the considerable uplift in a visitor experience as a result of these encounters. It has been scientifically proven that there is a direct correlation between random acts of kindness and happiness in a destination. So, a mantra for great tourist experiences is to make kindness the norm. We need to be RAKCTIVISTS.

> It has been scientifically proven that there is a direct correlation between random acts of kindness and happiness in a destination.

The Man Who Measures Clouds by Jan Fabre, Arsac Wine Experience, Bordeaux. Photo: Shutterstock.

Bergamo Città Alta. Photo: Shutterstock.

9. THE INSTITUTE OF RE-IMAGINED PLACES & EXPERIENCES INAUGURAL HALL OF FAME 2025

In 1986, the Northern Irish singer/songwriter Van Morrison released the album *No Guru, No Method, No Teacher*. The title deflects the idea that we should have a Hall of Fame. The title is evocative of a 1966 quotation by the Indian philosopher Jiddu Krishnamurti: 'there is no teacher, no pupil; there is no leader; there is no guru; there is no Master, no Saviour. You yourself are the teacher and the pupil; you are the Master; you are the guru; you are the leader; you are everything.'

This means that YOU, the reader, have the power and the potential to create the new types of tourist experiences defined in this book in the same way as these inductees into the inaugural, albeit virtual, Hall of Fame have boldly pushed the boundaries as to what can be achieved.

This is our tribute to 18 individuals. These are the alchemists, people who have transformed or created something through a magical process, and by doing so have deeply influenced the way we should all think about curating exceptional places, spaces, encounters and experiences for guest and host interactions. Their inclusion reflects their commitment to challenging traditional perspectives and ways of seeing; their bravery to try something new, often against all the odds; and their modesty and self-deprecation in accepting that what they have done has made a DIFFERENCE. Some have sadly departed, whilst others are very much still driving forward with new ways of thinking.

Our 18 inaugural inductees for 2025 are from 10 different territories – from Norway to South Africa and from the USA to Slovenia.

KOOS BEKKER & KAREN ROOS is an inspirational partnership. They are the couple whose considerable global perspective, wealth, vision and expertise in the worlds of business and design have allowed them to experiment with reimagining and redefining hospitality experiences. At Babylonstoren in the Western Cape of South Africa they have created a unique and immersive experience that combines the charm of a historic farm with modern luxury and a focus on the natural beauty of the surrounding landscape. This model has now been deployed at The Newt in Somerset (England), creating a new benchmark in the quality of guest experiences based on reimagining sustainable land management with exquisite guest experiences.

The Newt. Photo: Terry Stevens.

FRANÇOIS DELAROZIÈRE is an engineering genius and the art director of La Machine, a creative company based in Nantes (France) that is a collaboration between artists, designers, fabricators and technicians. The company specialises in producing giant performing machines, often based on fantastical creatures, such as Le Grand Èlèphant. From 1987 he collaborated with Jean-Luc Courcoult in Royal de Luxe, the French street theatre company, bringing an exciting new dimension to place animation. His work, influenced by Leonardo da Vinci, Jules Verne, Gustave Eiffel, Antonio Gaudi, surrealism and dadaism, has been described as 'the nexus between Jules Verne via Leonardo and Heath Robinson'.

Photo: La Machine.

PETER FREEMAN is an enthusiast who uniquely worked in four English National Parks, pioneering such projects as the template for the original Ordnance Survey Leisure Map (Peak District), administering the largest UK guided walk programme (Dartmoor), best-selling walking guides (Northumberland) and the first national Mountain Weather Forecast (Lake District). He believes that environmental interpretation should be practical and useful as well as imaginative and inspiring if long-term support from local, visitor and government was to be maintained. A life-long mountaineer and landscape photographer, his 2008 book *Shadows of a Changing Land* is a portrait of two cherished National Parks.

Above: High Nick Cup, Appleby-in-Westmorland, England.
Photo: Peter Freeman.

SHADOWS OF A CHANGING LAND

The Spark and a Sense of Wonder

K.R. MANFRED GRUBAUER is a successful businessman (K.R. in Austria means Councillor of Commerce), former bar and restaurant owner and, until recently, the long-standing Chair of Linz Tourismus – one of the most coherent, effective and efficient destination management organisations in Europe. His ability to transform the citizens of Linz's ambivalent relationship with tourism to one where today the city, post European Capital of Culture in 2009, is proud and very positive of its reputation as one of the leading tourism destinations on the Danube.

Photo: Manfred Grubauer.

HALL OF FAME 2025

DENIS IVOŠEVIĆ is the Director of the Istrian Tourist Board. He has been one of the most important forces in harnessing tourism, agriculture, culture and gastronomy to regenerate, reimagine and reposition Croatian Istria over the past 20 years as a premium experience-focused destination following the years of post-conflict abandonment of the rural hinterland. His enthusiasm and understanding of the need for collaboration is infectious. It has made Istria a benchmark for contemporary sustainable tourism and unique, innovative, hyper-local experiences.

Photo: Visit Istria.

JANE JACOBS was a much-celebrated urban writer and activist who championed new community-based approaches to planning for over 40 years. Her 1961 treatise *The Death and Life of Great American Cities* became one of the most influential texts about the workings and failings of cities, inspiring generations of urban planners. She had no professional training in the field of city planning; instead, she relied on her observations and common sense to show why certain places work and what can be done to improve those that do not.

Photo: Creative Commons.

KLEMEN LANGUS is the energetic force, ringmaster and visionary Director of the award-winning Bohinj Tourist Board in the Julian Alps of Slovenia. He, together with a small collective of like-minded professionals, including the inspirational Eva Štravs Podlogar, have formed the Julian Alps Association to pursue the achievement of the UN Sustainable Development Goals by defining the caring capacity for the destination (not its carrying capacity). Together, they have developed the clever concept of telling visitors that 'This is our living room – welcome to our home and explore our way of life in a reciprocal, respectful, manner.' It is a concept applicable to every destination.

Photo: Klemen Langus.

LUCY R. LIPPARD is an award-winning, internationally known American writer, art critic, activist and curator. Among her many books on contemporary and feminist art are two seminal works on tourism, art and place: *Off The Beaten Track* (1999) and *The Lure of the Local: Senses of Place in a Multicentered Society* (1997). Together, they provide a foundation for experience development, brimming full of wisdom, ideas and so much common sense.

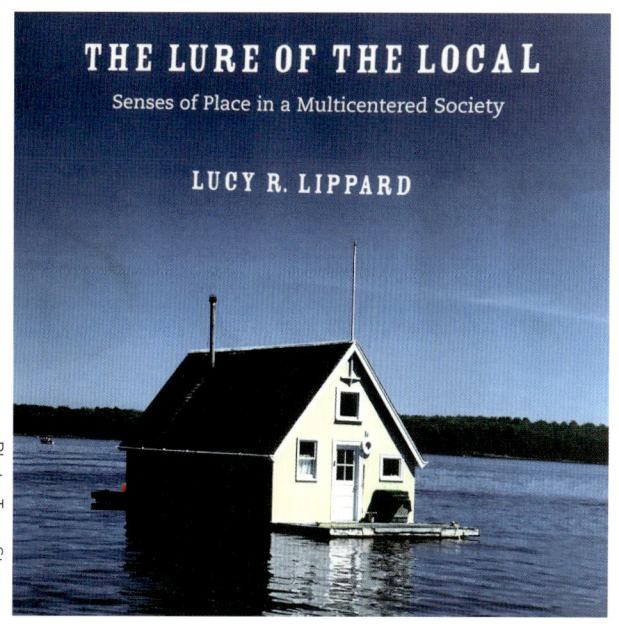

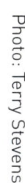

ANITA MENDIRATTA is a Canadian-born global tourism management specialist whose enduring focus has been on why we travel, the activation of meaningful experiences and empowering communities. Her 2011 book *Come Closer: How Tourism is Shaping the Future of Nations* is a significant statement of her convictions and her status as a highly respected ambassador for travel and tourism. Her advocacy for greater understanding and interaction between host and guest has been consistently deployed around the world, and her most recent book, *A Call to Leadership: Unlocking the Leader Within in Times of Crisis*, is prescient and directional.

MSc MAJA PAK OLAJ is the highly regarded Director of the Slovenian Tourist Board (STB). She has dedicated her career to Slovenian tourism and been a central and consistent figure in Slovenia's successful emergence as a world leader in sustainable and responsible tourism. Under her leadership, the STB has become the benchmark for a national tourism organisation. With her keen background in research, analytics and strategic planning, she has driven the green, boutique and experience agenda to new levels, allowing the country of just 2 million people to be in the vanguard of leading destinations in the world. The Slovenian Unique Experiences are a global benchmark for anyone considering how to create and how to enjoy connecting people, place through wonderful stories.

PATRICK TORRENT QUELL graduated in both industrial psychology and in law. He started his professional career in the financial sector, but for over 30 years has been central to transforming the way we think about strategic and sustainable tourism development. He is now the Executive Director of the Catalan Tourist Board and, since 2015, has represented Catalunya in NECSTouR, where he became the President of this network of regional tourism authorities from across Europe. He is a quiet, modest and inspirational leader whose impact on the way we need to think about sustainable tourism and experience development goes far beyond his beloved Catalunya. It is an approach that is truly significant in deepening our understanding and appreciation of the culture of Catalonia.

CLAUS SENDLINGER has been called 'the perpetual transformer always seeking to evolve hospitality'. He is a true visionary. From modest beginnings working in the PR department of the German Air Force, he entered the world of tourism by acquiring a travel agency aged just 23. After his creation of Design Hotels in the early '90s – a move that anointed the relationship between hotels, design and life-centred guest experiences – he is now leading his Slowness team to reimagine the next era in hospitality. He is setting out how we can reconnect with places, people and ideas in ways that feel grounded and real, an experiment which is being pursued in his new project, the Flussbad Campus in Berlin. He says, 'It will be an exploration of how Slowness's life-centered philosophy honours the connections between all living things and strengthens the bonds between them.'

Photo: Clemens Poloczek.

HALL OF FAME 2025

ESENCAN TERZIBASOGLU joined the UN World Tourism Organisation (now UN Tourism) in 2001 with responsibility for supervising and running the programme initiatives in the area of tourism destination management. She enthusiastically and expertly promoted the concept, especially at the regional and local levels. The quality of the visitor experience together with effective sustainable destination governance was at the heart of everything she did. She studied urban and regional planning at the Middle East Technical University in Tűrkiye and enjoyed a career in the country's tourism industry before joining the UNWTO. Her tenacity and passion for effective experience-based destination management is infectious and compelling. She has inspired many.

Photo: Terry Stevens.

FREEMAN TILDEN (1883–1980), who was born in Massachusetts, set down the principles and theories of heritage and environmental interpretation. His work with the United States National Park Service inspired generations of interpreters across the world. Tilden's quotations (from his definitive 1957 book *Interpreting Our Heritage*) are the most cited phrases on the subject of communicating with visitors. They include 'Put there just a spark' and 'Through interpretation, understanding; through understanding, appreciation; through appreciation, protection.'

TORUNN TRONSVANG is the founder of UpNorway, a company designed to fulfil the most thoughtful travellers' interest in experiences off the beaten path and closer to heart in terms of authenticity, involvement and connection, thus creating better practices in ecotourism and responsible social impact. By recognising the new responsible and empathetic traveller, she presents authentic culture at its best by introducing tourists to warm and genuine people who take pride in what they do and where they come from; who'll treat our traveller as a guest rather than a customer.

K.R. SUSANNE KRAUS-WINKLER

is a longstanding entrepreneur and industry representative in the hospitality industry, with 40 years of practical experience, and a founding partner of the LOISIUM Wine & Spa Resort Hotel Group. The Loisium experience epitomises their location, celebrating the place and its heritage. She has held positions on the management board of tourism organisations in Austria and at EU level as well as President of the Austrian Professional Hotel Association. From July 2022 until Spring 2025, Susanne served as Austria's State Secretary for Tourism. In that role she successfully focused on sustainability, digitalisation and the labour market. She has now returned to her entrepreneurial role, ensuring Austria's continued leading role in global tourism.

Photo: Susanne Kraus-Winkler.

HALL OF FAME 2025

GORDON YOUNG glories in being a Leeds United fan. Born in Carlisle, this rebellious, often dogmatic artist specialises in public art, including typographical elements, and has had a transformational impact on all the places he has worked. His *Comedy Carpet* on Blackpool Promenade (2011) is said to be the largest piece of public art in Britain. It makes you laugh; it makes you cry; it makes you think. He was curator of the wondrous Yorkshire Sculpture Park and director of the Welsh Sculpture Trust before becoming a full-time artist creating installations that demand attention and provoke enquiry – for example, *The Mystery of the Seven Stanes* (Scotland), *Fish Pavement* (Hull) and *A Flock of Words* (Morecambe). He challenges us to think 'outside of the box'.

Photo: Gordon Young Associates.

TRINE KANTER ZERWEKH is Senior Advisor to the Norwegian Public Road Administration for the ongoing development of the Nasjonale Turistveger/ Norwegian Scenic Routes project, which has its origins in 1993. The project is designed to provide places for travellers to rest, immerse themselves in and reflect upon the extraordinary landscapes. Art and architecture add an extra dimension, stimulating the traveller to reflect upon their connections with the environment. Today, there are 18 routes with 185 installations that enhance the wonderment and awe of the Norwegian scenery. It has been her determination and eye for detail that has ensured these experiences deliver wonder, admiration and that all-important awe factor.

The Tower of Health and Joy, Podčetrtek, Slovenia. Photo: Slovenian Tourist Board.

88   The Spark and a Sense of Wonder

10. MY BACK PAGES – SOME FINAL THOUGHTS BY TERRY STEVENS

Van Morrison tells us that 'Precious time is slipping away', whilst in his song 'Dweller on the Threshold', as Emonn Hughes writes in the preface to *Lit Up Inside: Selected Lyrics*: **'Morrison is talking for all of us, poised throughout our lives between what we have already experienced and what may lay ahead.'**

These are challenging times for the future of tourism and, as Bob Dylan reminds us, 'you don't need a weatherman to tell you which way the wind is blowin'.' Certainly, the wisdom is needed as never before that I (we) 'was so much older then, we are younger than that now.'

In 1966, Keef Relf (of The Yardbirds) implored us to be courageous, 'Will time make man more wise, now the trees are almost green? When time and tides have been, will I be bolder than today?'

Can we all be bolder and allow ourselves to rise to the visitors' demand, described by Rosa Park (founder of *Cereal Travel* magazine): 'we want to feel as if we are in on the locals' secret or, better, we want to fully engage with that activity, not simply be an observer.'

This means a more flexible approach, more creativity, greater improvisation to do what Claus Sendlinger (writing in *Directions*, Issue 14, 2018) described as 'the creation of a place where there is meaningful exchange. Only then are you serving an authentic desire and bringing a community together with the visitor through shared, often highly socialised, experiences. Why not think things that have never been thought of before?'

This means that the tourism planners of tomorrow need to be willing to be more pirate – more rebellious. For Jane Jacobs, it was for us to create in our destinations a 'sidewalk ballet' where the nights are as interesting as the days and where the days are as much fun as the nights. For the Finnish architect and designer Alvar Aalto, 'radicalism is required so that superficial cosiness can be avoided. In its place pin down the problems whose solutions we will create forming the basis of the values for the well-being of man that are genuinely worthy of development.'

Unique ski craftsman. Photo: Marion Luttenberger, Tourismus Vienna.

It's not just the new generation of tourism planners who need to heed this advice. T. S. Eliot observed that 'we must not cease from exploration and the end of all our exploring will be to arrive where we began and to know the place for the first time.' The exhortation is evident in his poem East Coker (from the *Four Quartets*) – a poem which is all about a sense of place and the sense of wonder.

It is Eliot's words in *The Definition of Culture* that takes us back to psychogeography and tourism: 'Men desire of their neighbours something sufficiently akin to be understood, something sufficiently different to provoke attention, and something great enough to command admiration.'

This implies the kind of Eutopia conceptualised by the Scottish biologist and pioneering town planner Patrick Geddes (1854–1932) and articulated by Graham King in personal correspondence, where he says, 'sense of place is governed by an experiential awareness of all our senses – the warm rain, the tang of a sea breeze, the cry of the seagulls – to know what feels good and what does not; and, walking, taking things slowly is essential. It is all about space and time.'

Unashamedly, I will end with a quotation from another 'son' of East Coker, who claims that curiosity is in us all and experiences should capture and satisfy the curious mind. William Dampier (1651–1715) was born in East Coker. At the age of 14 he left the village to begin a celebrated and oft-times flawed life as a buccaneer, explorer and hydrographer who circumnavigated the world three times and was the first Englishman to map Australia. Known as the 'Pirate with the Exquisite Mind', he wrote, 'A lack of prejudice and an inextinguishable curiosity makes one an instinctive traveller.' Let us all ensure that this curiosity is given the spark to ignite it and the sense of place to nurture and feed it.

In his 2005 biopic *No Direction Home*, Bob Dylan refers to himself as a music expeditionary. We should all become a tourism experience expeditionary – a leader of change in a complex, anonymous, digitalised world?

So, it all begins with a spark! For Freeman Tilden the mantra was always that our job is to generate a spark to ignite curiosity. Bruce Springsteen recognised that you can't start a fire without a spark. Angela Ahrendts alerts us to the role of leaders of change nurturing the spark of interest in colleagues. Great experiences begin with a spark… to ignite, nurture and fuel future visitor experiences.

That requires both the creators and the consumers of great experiences to be open-minded – Frank Zappa pronounced, 'the mind is like a parachute. It doesn't work if it is not open.' And, as leaders of change, those of us involved in curating guest experiences must be bold and brave.

According to Jerry Garcia of the Grateful Dead, as quoted in *Marketing Lessons from the Grateful Dead* (2010), this requires of us all not simply to strive to be the best of the best but to be the only ones that do what you do, especially when celebrating unique sense of place through great experiences. It's no longer about the 'wow' but rather the 'awe' and that sense of wonder.

And finally, finally… remember that there are only two rules in tourism.

Rule 1: Always deliver great, unique, memorable experiences.

Rule 2: Never forget Rule 1.

Graffiti at Ars Electronica Festival, Linz. Photo: Terry Stevens.

11. THE RESOURCES

A GREAT LISTEN: THE PSYCHOGEOGRAPHICAL TOP 20 PLAYLIST: MUSIC TO PROVOKE NEW THINKING

Forget the Wi-Fi. Get out the Hi-Fi. Put on the vinyl. Sit back and listen.

- *Midnight Rambler* – Rolling Stones
- *Like a Rolling Stone* – Bob Dylan
- *I go Walkin's After Midnight* – Patsy Cline
- *Walking By The River* – Ella Fitzgerald
- *Free Man in Paris* – Joni Mitchell
- *Ramble On* – Led Zeppelin
- *Ramblin' on my Mind* – Robert Johnston
- *Ramble on Rose* – Grateful Dead
- *Ramblin's Round* – Arlo Guthrie
- *Rambling* – Aretha Franklin
- *Take it Easy* – Eagles
- *Hyndford Street* – Van Morrison
- *Into The Mystic* – Van Morrison
- *Walking Blues* – Son House
- *Stairway to Heaven* – Led Zeppelin
- *Life's What You Make It* – Talk Talk
- *Wonderous Stories* – Yes
- *Nagorny Karabach* – Einstürzende Neubauten
- *Learning to Fly* – Pink Floyd
- *Walking Down The Road* – The Ozark Mountain Daredevils
- *Gwesty Cymru (Does neb yn talu)* – Geraint Jarman
- *Hen Ffordd Gymreig O Fyw* – Edward H. Dafis

A GREAT READ: THE INSTITUTE'S SUGGESTED READING LIST

Monumento all'Alpino, Torri del Benaco, Lake Garda, Italy. Photo: Terry Stevens.

Allende, S. C. (2018) *Be More Pirate*. Portfolio Penguin. London.

Antoniou, A. (2015) *Mind The Map*. Gestalten. Berlin.

Brown, M. and Davies, R. (2021). *Atlas of Imagined Places*. Batsford. London.

Carson. R. (1962) *Silent Spring*. Houghton Mifflin.

Carson, R. (1965/1998) *A Sense of Wonder*. Harper & Row/Harper Collins.

Davies, P. and Knipe, T. (1984) *A Sense of Place*. Sunderland Arts Centre Ltd.

Davies, W. H. (2010) *The Autobiography of a Super-Tramp*. London. Amberley Publishing.

Debord, G. (1959) *Theory of the Dérive* in the *Situationist International Anthology*. Translated by

Knabb, K. and published by The Bureau of Public Secrets in 2006.

De Botton, A. (2002) *The Art of Travel*. Hamish Hamilton by Penguin. London.

DeLana, L. (2021) *Do/Walk/: Navigate earth, mind and body. Step by step*. Do Book Co. Work in Progress Publishing.

De Quincey, T. (1821) *Confessions of an English Opium-Eater*. London. J.B. Alden.

Eliot, T. S. (2001) *Four Quartets*. London. Faber & Faber.

Filep, S. and Pearce, P. (ed) (2014) *Tourist Experiences and Fulfilment: Insights from Positive Psychology*. Routledge. London.

Fleming, R, L. (2007) *The Art of Placemaking: Interpreting Community Through Public Art and Urban Design*. Merrell. New York.

Ginsburg, A. (1967) *Wales Visitation*

Gros, F. (2015) *A Philosophy of Walking*. Verso.

Gunn, Clare A. (1972) *Vacationscape: Designing Tourist Regions*. University of Texas. Austin.

Hardy, T. (1974) *The Woodlanders*. London. Macmillan.

Henderson, C. (2017) *A New Map of Wonders*. London. Granta.

Henry, J. and Anthony, R. (2005) *The Lonely Planet Guide to Experiential Travel*. Footscray. Australia.

Hodge and Perisighetti et al. (2006) *A Mis-guide to Anywhere*. Wrights & Sites. London.

IEDC (2014) *A Creative Environment for Creative Leadership*. Bled. Slovenia.

Johnson, S. (2010) *Where Do Good Ideas Come From: The Natural History of Innovation*. Allen Lane. New York

Kazin, A. (1988) *A Writer's America: Landscape in Literature*. New York. Knopf Publishing.

Kerouac, J. (1957) *On The Road*. New York. Penguin.

King. G.A.K. (2017) *PG1 + PG2 Psychogeography & Town Planning: An Exploration by a Swansea Planner*.

Personal Correspondence. March.

Lee, L. (1969) *As I Walked Out One Midsummer Morning*. London. Penguin.

Lippard, L.R. (1997) *The Lure of the Local: Sense of Place in a Multicentered Society*. The New Press. New York.

Lois-González, R. et al. (2014) *New Tourism in the 21st Century: Culture, the City, Nature and Spirituality*. Cambridge Scholars Publishing.

Machen, A. (1924) *The London Adventure, or The Art of Wandering*. London. Tartarus Press.

Malpas, J. (2018). *Place and Experience: A Philosophical Topography*. 2nd, rev. ed. London: Routledge, 2018. First published 1999, by Cambridge University Press.

Mendiratta, A. (2011) *Come Closer: How Tourism is Shaping the Future of Nations*. Myriad Publishing. South Africa.

Mendiratta, A. (2023) *The Call to Leadership: Unlocking the Leader Within in Times of Crisis*. Anita Mendiratta Foundation. London.

Nairn, I. (1955) *Outrage*. The Architectural Press. London.

National Public Roads Administration (2023) *Nasjonale Turistveger*. Oslo, Norway.

Prebensen, N et al (Eds) (2014) *Creating Experience Value in Tourism*. Oxford. CABI.

Pirsig, R. (1974) *Zen and The Art of Motorcycle Maintenance*. New York. Morrow Publishing.

Reuters Photographers (2004) *On The Road: The Art of The Journey*. New York.

Self, W. (2013) *Psychogeography*. London. Bloomsbury.

Sinclair, I. (1997) *Lights Out for the Territory*. Granta. London.

Solnit, R. (2001) *Wanderlust: A History of Walking*. VERSO. London.

Steinbeck, J. (1932) *The Pastures of Heaven*. London. Penguin.

Swift, J. (1756) *Gulliver's Travels*. London. Benjamin Motte.

Stevens, T. (2023) *Wish You Were Here. The stories behind 50 of Europe's great destinations*. Cardiff. Graffeg.

Stevens, T. (2024) *Bucked in the Yarn: The Unique Heritage of Coker Canvas*. Cardiff. Graffeg.

Stevenson, R. L. (2004) *Travels with a Donkey in the Cévennes*. London. Penguin. Originally published in 1897 by Chatto & Windus.

Tilden F. (1957) *Interpreting Our Heritage*. Chapel Hill.

Urry, J. (1990) *The Tourist Gaze: Leisure and Travel in Contemporary Societies*. London. SAGE Publications.

Varlow, S. (1996) *A Reader's Guide to Writers' Britain*. Andre Deutsch Publishing.

Verne, J. (Various) *Around the World in Eighty Days*. London. Simon & Schuster.

NOTHING GREAT IN THE WORLD HAS EVER BEEN ACCOMPLISHED WITHOUT PASSION.

GEORG WILHELM FRIEDRICH HEGEL, GERMAN IDEALIST (1770–1831)

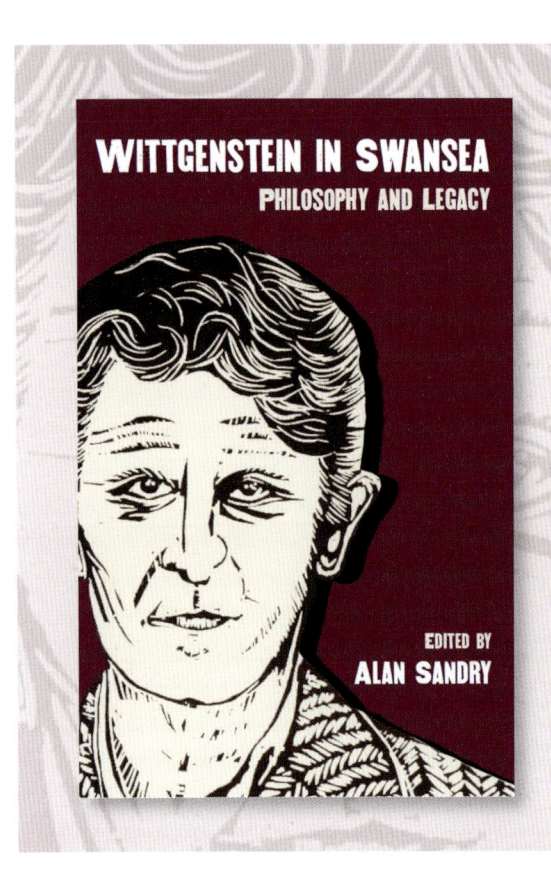

Wittgenstein in Swansea
Philosophy and Legacy

Aspects of Ludwig Wittgenstein's time in Swansea between 1942 and 1947 with views on his philosophy and legacy from different perspectives and some psychogeographical observations of the philosopher's present-day significance to Swansea.

Published by University of Wales Press/Gwasg Prifysgol Cymru

Paperback 9781837722259
eBook pdf 9781837722266
eBook epub 978183772227

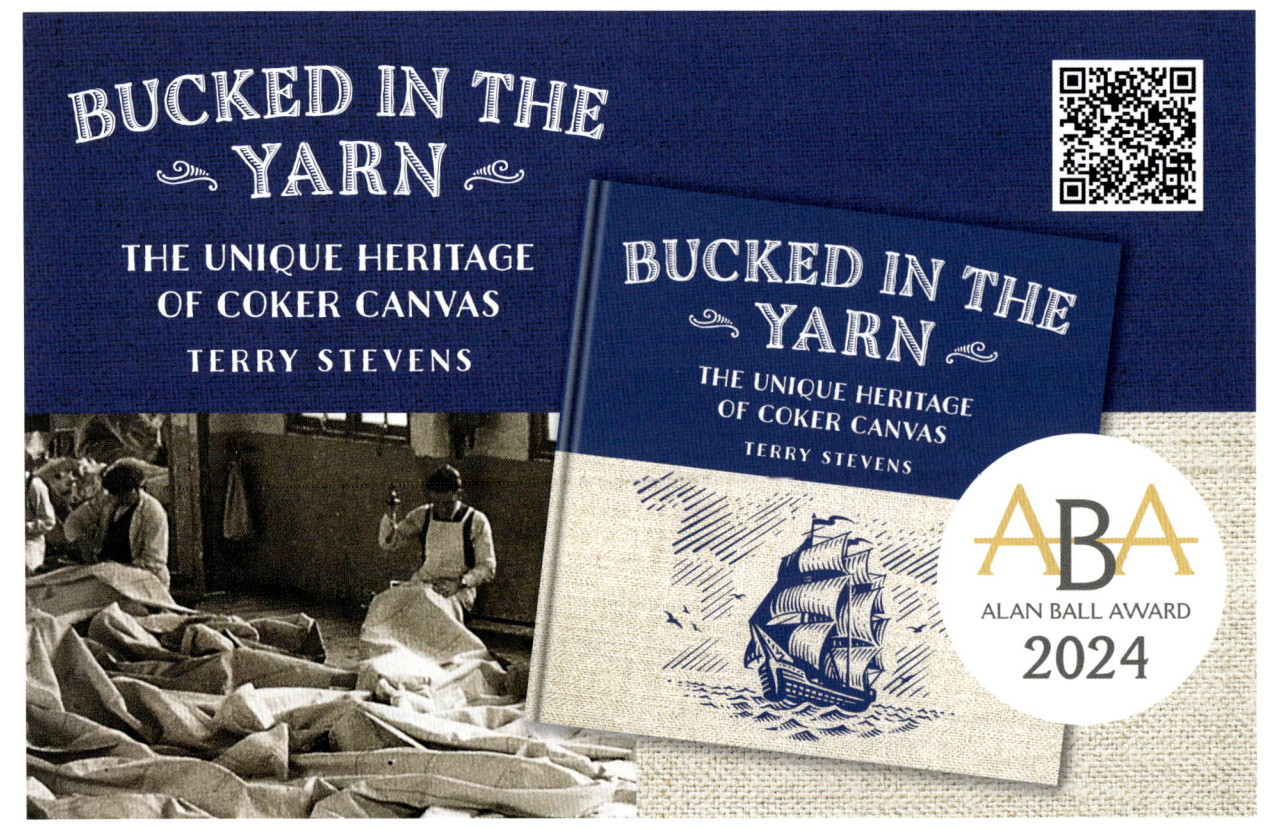

BUCKED IN THE YARN
THE UNIQUE HERITAGE OF COKER CANVAS
TERRY STEVENS

ABA ALAN BALL AWARD 2024

CATALUNYA

Catalonia is appetising

WORLD REGION OF GASTRONOMY
CATALONIA AWARDED 2025

Generalitat de Catalunya
Government of Catalonia

Fáilte Feirste Thiar
PROMOTING WEST BELFAST TOURISM
www.visitwestbelfast.com

"EXPERIENCE THE CULTURAL HEARTBEAT OF BELFAST"
www.visitwestbelfast.com

'Books that put a zoom lens of destinations and their leaders analysing what it takes for a destination to build and rebuild for success.'

ANITA MENDIRATTA, SPECIAL ADVISER TO UN TOURISM

'These books give destinations a real world context, their personality, their mood, how to understand these places and experience them.'

PETER GREENBERG, TRAVEL EDITOR CBS NEWS

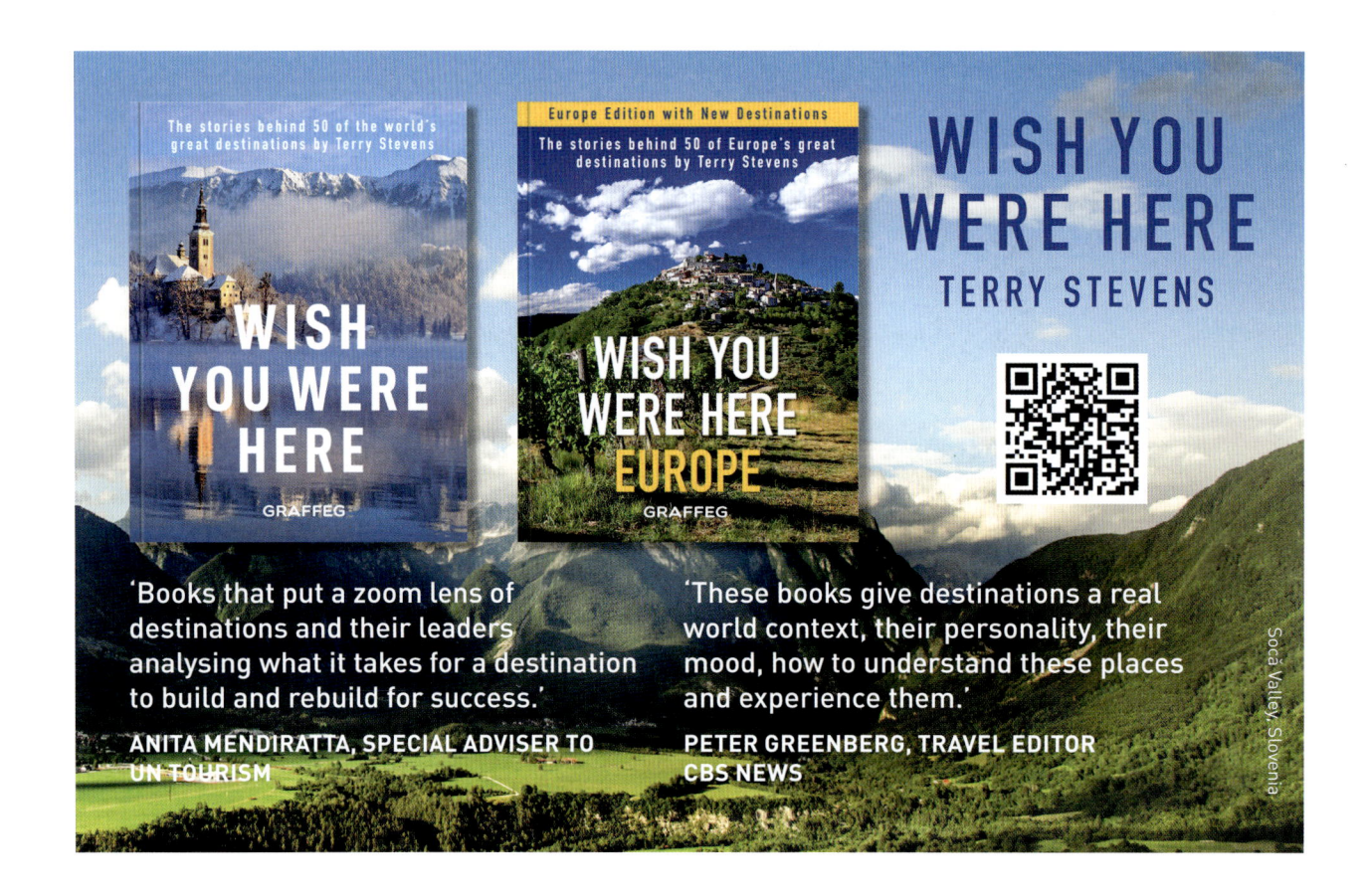

The Spark and a Sense of Wonder
Published in Great Britain in 2025 by Graffeg Limited.
ISBN 9781805950554

Text by Terry Stevens copyright © 2025.
Designed and produced by Graffeg Limited copyright © 2025.

Graffeg Limited, 15 Neptune Court, Vanguard Way, Cardiff, CF24 5PJ, Wales, UK. Tel: 01554 824000. croeso@graffeg.com. www.graffeg.com.

Terry Stevens is hereby identified as the author of this work in accordance with section 77 of the Copyright, Designs and Patents Act 1988.

Printed by FINIDR, s.r.o., Czechia.

A CIP Catalogue record for this book is available from the British Library.

All rights reserved. No part of this publication may be reproduced, stored in a retrieval system or transmitted, in any form or by any means, electronic, mechanical, photocopying, recording or otherwise, without the prior permission of the publishers.

This book is designed for general readers, printed with materials and processes that are safe and meet all applicable European safety requirements. The book does not contain elements that could pose health or safety risks under normal and intended use.

We hereby declare that this product complies with all applicable requirements of the General Product Safety Regulation (GPSR) and any other relevant EU legislation.

Appointed EU Representative:
Easy Access System Europe Oü, 16879218
Mustamäe tee 50, 10621, Tallinn, Estonia
gpsr.requests@easproject.com

Every effort has been made to trace copyright holders of material and acknowledge permission for this publication. The publisher apologises for any errors or omissions to rights holders and would be grateful for notification of credits and corrections that should be included in future reprints or editions of this book.

1 2 3 4 5 6 7 8 9